1997

ELEPHANTS

A Battle for Survival

Lisa Lawley

HEADLINE

A FRIEDMAN GROUP BOOK

Copyright © 1991 Michael Friedman Publishing Group, Inc.

First published in Great Britain in 1991
by HEADLINE BOOK PUBLISHING PLC

British Library Cataloguing-in-Publication Data
Lawley, Lisa
Elephants.
1. Elephants
I. Title
599.61

ISBN 0-7472-0377-6

ELEPHANTS
A Battle for Survival
was prepared and produced by
Michael Friedman Publishing Group, Inc.
15 West 26th Street
New York, New York 10010

Editor: Elizabeth Viscott Sullivan
Art Director: Jeff Batzli
Designer: Kevin Ullrich
Photography Editor: Anne K. Price

Typeset by Bookworks Plus
Color separation by Scantrans Pte. Ltd.
Printed and bound in Hong Kong by Leefung-Asco Printers Ltd.

HEADLINE BOOK PUBLISHING PLC
Headline House
79 Great Titchfield Street
London W1P 7FN

Additional Photo Credits
Page 1 © Lee Kuhn/FPG International, Page 2-3 © Gerry Ellis/
The Wildlife Collection, Page 6 © Stephen J. Krasemann/
Valan Photos, Page 7 © Art Resource

DEDICATION

For my parents, who tell of one of my first forays into the world of

speech, an ambitious attempt to sound the name *elephant,*

and for George, who said jump

ACKNOWLEDGEMENTS

For their gifts of encouragement I owe a tremendous debt to Terry

Kay, Bill Winn, Gage Johnston, Maria Bottino, and Jessica Mitchell.

To all who offered support and information during the researching

and writing of this book, I offer my deepest thanks, especially to

Amy Boorstein, George Butler, Ann Cahn, David Groff, Ann Hessey,

John Kagwi, Muhoho Kenyatta, George Nesbitt, Dr. James and

Mrs. Mary Nesbitt, Peter Riva, Jennifer Smith, Laurie Stark,

Geraldine Stutz, Steve Topping, Victoria Wilson, the late Eric Woodley,

and Ruth Woodley. And finally, I thank my editors, Melissa Schwarz

and Liz Sullivan, for their confidence, discernment, and suggestions,

without which this book would not be.

CONTENTS

chapter one

A CREATURE FROM THE PAST

Six blind men of Hindustan . . . wanted to find out what an elephant was like and quarrelled over their conclusions after meeting one for the first time. The first, stumbling against its side, thought that the elephant must be like a wall; the second, feeling the tusks, assumed it was like a spear; the third, holding the trunk, was sure it was like a snake; the fourth, stroking the leg, knew it was like a tree; the fifth, examining the ears, considered it was like a fan; and the last man, grabbing the tail, could tell that the elephant was like a rope.

S. K. Eltringham, **Elephants**

The often-repeated Indian proverb of the blind men and the elephant is usually intended as a reminder of the folly of leaping to conclusions based on insufficient information. But the story equally serves as an inventory of the motley collection of features that makes an elephant . . . well, an *elephant.* This rare combination of assets makes the elephant instantly recognizable the world over, popular among children and adults, and the inspiration alternately for fear, laughter, awe, and a very healthy measure of respect. Wherever on earth it has been found, the elephant has exerted a tremendous influence over humans, who have loved and hunted, revered and slaughtered, pampered and then recklessly consumed these creatures with a ferocity and ambivalence shown perhaps to no other animal.

Most spectacular, and certainly most obvious, is the elephant's enormous size, a characteristic that renders it invulnerable (except for the

Opposite page: The elephant, the largest land mammal now walking the earth, never ceases to fascinate its human observers. Its special anatomical features, including the unique trunk, are the result of millions of years of adaptation to the environments of Africa and Asia.

The Asian elephant's ears, much smaller than the ears of its African cousin, often curl toward the front as the animal grows older. The Asian's double-domed forehead is another feature that distinguishes it from the African elephant. Asian females usually do not bear visible tusks, and many males are also tuskless.

very young) to all living creatures except humans. Its gargantuan ears, which serve a very important role in temperature regulation, make the not-particularly-fleet-footed elephant look as if it could—*almost*—take wing and fly, like Dumbo, the cartoon elephant of Walt Disney fame. The elephant's tusks, greatly coveted by humans, are by far longer and more elegant than those of the few other animals that also have them. And the elephant's flexible, endlessly useful trunk, a lithe appendage that is nose and lip combined, has no equivalent feature in any other animal. Yet the stately elephant sports on its ample backside a skinny little fly whisk of a tail. Improbable as the elephant's parts are, the whole is a creature of consummate dignity, or of wicked hilarity, depending upon the individual elephant's mood and personality. In addition to its superb equipment for managing its physical environment, the elephant is keenly intelligent and emotionally complex in a way that resembles no other animal so much as man.

The elephant is truly king of beasts in mind, body, and soul; but more than that, it and its relatives have displayed impressive staying power over the millenia. Although only two species of elephant, the Asian (*Elephas maximus*) and the African (*Loxodonta africana*) survive today, the zoological order *Proboscidea* (meaning "animals with trunks"), composed of creatures known to have been in some way similar to our elephants, includes some 350 species altogether. During the last 50 million years, since the first ancestral elephants emerged in the Eocene epoch, members of *Proboscidea* spread from their birthplaces in northeastern Africa over most of the planet, with the notable exceptions of Antarctica and Australia.

ELEPHANT ANCESTORS

Before there were elephants, the world saw a succession of creatures that seem to have been early relatives, although these animals most likely were not direct ancestors. One of these was the *Moeritherium,* whose fossilized remains from the Eocene epoch (52 million to 37 million years ago) have been unearthed in Africa. The *Moeritherium* was a small, possibly hippopotamuslike creature that is believed to have dwelled in prehistoric swamps. This early *Proboscidean* must have been less than happy straddling the fence between the worlds of water and land, for perhaps 30 million years ago, in the Oligocene epoch, the *Moeritherium* seems to have diverged into several distinct lines. One of these lines led to the emergence of a group of wholly aquatic creatures, known today variously as sea cows, manatees, and dugongs. Another line evolved into the small, squirrelly-looking creatures known as hyraxes. In fact, the hyrax, in spite of its furry body and diminutive size, is considered the elephant's closest living relative because of the many subtle anatomical features the two animals share. Chief among these is an extraordinarily lengthy gestation period (about twenty-two months, as compared with a human's nine) and the location of the males' testicles within the abdominal cavity; the latter feature is unique to these two species among mammals, whose high internal temperatures are usually destructive to sperm.

Another elephant relative, the *Deinotherium,* probably made its appearance in the late Miocene epoch (which lasted from 27 million to 13 million years ago), as the earth commenced a period of cooling. *Deinotherium*s were as large, some even larger, than today's elephants, and they traversed Africa and Europe for some 15 million years without undergoing any great evolutionary change before they slipped into extinction. Scientists' re-creations of the *Deinotherium* suggest a build that was something of a cross between the elephant, the rhinoceros, and the hippopotamus. Because its nasal cavities were located high in its skull, the *Deinotherium* presumably had a true trunk, rather than a somewhat elongated snout such as the *Moeritherium* may have had. This organ developed as an implement to help the animal gather enough food, probably in response to increasing body size, which raised the position of the animal's head above the level of the most plentiful plant matter. The *Deinotherium*'s tusks, most unlike an elephant's, were rooted in the lower jaw and curved downward. One theory suggests that these odd tusks may have been used to scrape together quantities of swamp vegetation, which were then eaten with the aid of the trunk.

The *Mammut,* or mastodon, whose remains are plentiful in the United States, also evolved in the Miocene epoch, but may have died out as recently as ten thousand years ago. Its skeleton, particularly the foreshortened, high-domed skull and the location of its huge, upward-curving tusks in the upper jaw, is very like that of our contemporary elephants. But the mastodon had yet to develop the abruptly shortened lower jaw that enables a true elephant's skull to function as a highly effective "first order" lever operated by the strong muscles joining the neck and the base of the skull.

This shortened lower jaw was an advantageous biological development, according to S. K. Eltringham's *Elephants,* because it reduced the amount of energy required to perform the task of eating. In the case of an animal with the elephant's bulk, which requires a lot of food to carry out its metabolic processes, it is important for the ratio between the amount of energy used to eat and the amount of energy derived from the vegetation it consumes to remain in proper balance.

Another clue that the mastodon's relation to today's elephants was a somewhat distant one can be found in its other name, *Mammut,* which

An African bush elephant bull may weigh a ton (.9 t) or more than its Asian counterpart. Its large, fanlike ears echo the shape of the continent where it resides.

The *Moeritherium*, a swamp-dwelling, distant ancestor of the elephant, is considered more closely related to the tiny hyrax and to a group of aquatic mammals that includes the dugong. Another distant elephant ancestor, the *Deinotherium*, probably had a trunk resembling the elephant's, but its tusks grew from the animal's lower jaw.

refers to the nipple-shaped projections on the surface of its teeth. In this characteristic, too, the mastodon was unlike the elephant, which developed a very specialized dentition, probably as a way of coping with the grasses that began to appear more frequently on its menu, replacing much of the softer, leafier vegetable matter its predecessors had enjoyed.

The suborder of *Proboscidea* called *Gomphotherioidea* contained several highly migratory creatures—the *Cuvieronius,* the *Haplomastodon,* and the *Stegotetrabelodon*—that made their way across Europe and Asia and passed over the land bridge that once connected Siberia with North America. From there they forged a path onward well into South America. Of these animals, the *Stegotetrabelodon,* classed in a subfamily of the Elephantidae, is considered to have been closely related to *Primelephas,* the progenitor of our modern-day elephants.

Primelephas appeared in Africa toward the end of the Miocene period, some 13 or 14 million years ago. In addition to its large size, trunk, upward curving tusks rooted in the upper jaw, and efficient skull/jaw mechanism that made bulk feeding practicable, *Primelephas* had a ridged molar on each side of its upper and lower jaw. When *Prim-*

Deinotherium

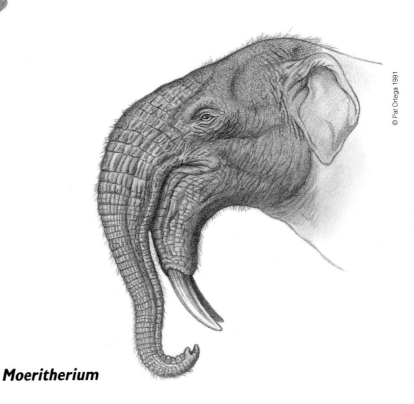

Moeritherium

elephas chewed, these ridged teeth fit together in a type of tongue-and-groove arrangement. This enabled the animal to slice or shear vegetable matter, particularly tough grasses, into easily digestible bits with a single backward-and-forward movement of the jaw. As each of these molars wore down, a new molar erupted in the back of the jaw and pushed forward to take the place of the old molar, which eventually broke up and fell out a flake at a time, just as elephant teeth still do today.

Later elephants, grouped in the genera *Loxodonta, Elephas,* and *Mamuthus,* exhibited only one major improvement in this special dental arrangement: the development of a high crown to the molars. This further improved the elephant's grazing efficiency, since the dental ridges were now deeper and the shearing surfaces longer. As far as scientists have been able to determine, this development was the final evolutionary mark of the elephant as we now know it. Elephants of these three genera continued to change in small ways in response to local conditions, but for the most part they were well equipped and ready to explore the vast territories of the globe.

The least fortunate of *Primelephas*'s descendants, *Mamuthus,* gradually migrated from Africa into Western Europe. From there, two species,

Mamuthus, progenitor of the three genera of true elephants, included many wide-ranging species, among them the woolly mammoth. Although these species closely resembled modern elephants, the *Mamuthus* line is now extinct. Scientists continue to puzzle over why these magnificent animals died out.

Mamuthus

Mamuthus primigenius (woolly mammoth)

© Pat Ortega 1991

University Museum, University of Pennsylvania

Above: This specimen of *Mamuthus primigenius*, or woolly mammoth, was discovered in Berezovka, Siberia. The mammoth's spiraled tusks are somewhat harder than those of modern elephants and almost twice as long.

Opposite page: Ivory poaching and sport hunting over several centuries have reduced the Asian elephant population to about forty-five thousand individuals in widely separated populations. The species faces a severe and ongoing threat in the form of habitat encroachment; a renewal of interest in its skin for use in manufacturing various handicrafts recently has intensified the danger of its extinction.

Mamuthus meridionalis (which soon died out) and *Mamuthus armeniacus,* moved in separate waves into what is now the Soviet Union, across Siberia, and eventually over the Bering Strait into North America. *Armeniacus* evolved during this migration into a new species, *Mamuthus primigenius*—the famous woolly mammoth—and another species related to *primigenius, Mamuthus columbi,* pushed its way as far south as El Salvador. The earth was in an ice age, and the woolly mammoth was well suited to the cold climates it encountered, having developed a thick skin and an insulating layer of fat, as well as a short, downy, red-brown undercoat of warm fur covered with longer, coarser hair. Its ears were relatively small, which would have conserved body heat, unlike those of surviving elephants that claim warmer habitats and need a large ear surface to help dispel heat. The woolly mammoth's huge spiraled tusks, about 16 feet (5 m) in length, were almost twice the size of the largest African elephant tusks; with a shoulder height of 15 feet (4.5 m), it stood a head taller as well.

We know these facts about the woolly mammoth, as well as many details of its diet, because of the large number of corpses preserved intact in the permafrost regions of Siberia. The species traditionally was thought to have suffered abrupt extinction at least ten thousand years ago as a result of some dramatic environmental change, possibly the end of the last ice age. More recently, scientists have postulated that human hunters may have contributed to the mammoth's demise. Because of its plentiful, well-preserved remains and obviously splendid adaptive capabilities, the woolly mammoth appears to have lived tantalizingly close to our own time. Although we consider the creatures extinct, more than one scientist, and perhaps every schoolchild, has been tempted to imagine that somewhere, someday, the woolly mammoth might be discovered alive in the uncharted wildernesses of Siberia, or that bioengineering techniques will eventually enable man to clone one of these majestic animals from a single perfectly preserved cell.

Like *Mamuthus, Elephas* followed a wide-ranging migratory path. It moved first over Africa, then headed north into Europe and as far east as India before pushing northward again through China and Siberia, and eastward as far as Japan and Java. With twenty-three extinct species known, *Elephas* showed far more genetic diversification over the course of its development than did either of the other two lines descended from *Primelephas.*

Today, there is just one heir to *Elephas*'s once mighty and varied line: the Asian elephant, or *Elephas maximus,* found in scattered pockets throughout much of the southern part of its ancestors' former range. The Asian elephant is in very serious decline, because of overhunting in the past, but also because of intensified competition with civilization

© Gerry Ellis/The Wildlife Collection

© Warren Garst/Tom Stack & Associates

The Asian elephant's head, obviously the apex of its body, and convex back are characteristics that distinguish it from the African elephant.

over habitat and a recent spate of illegal trade in elephant skin products. Remnant herds, at most forty-five thousand animals in all, can be found in India, Myanmar, China, Thailand, Cambodia, Vietnam, Laos, Borneo, Malaya, Sri Lanka, Sumatra, and the Andaman Islands.

The descendants of *Loxodonta* have changed least during their tenure, choosing to remain in Africa, the continent of their origin. The question that most puzzles scientists studying the history of *Loxodonta* has to do with why the species *africana,* rather than *adaurora* (which fossils suggest was anatomically superior), has survived to the present day. *Loxodonta africana,* the African elephant, actually includes two subspecies: *Loxodonta africana africana,* the larger of the two, is the African elephant of the bush and plains, while *Loxodonta africana cyclotis,* adapted to forest and mountainous areas, has straighter tusks, smaller, more rounded ears, and a smaller overall build.

Humans have persistently hunted the African elephant for thousands of years, but the animals managed to survive in relatively large numbers until the last decade. During the 1980s, the African elephant population was halved, largely through poaching, and there may now be no more than 600,000 members of the species remaining. The African elephant has been extinct in North Africa—the victim of the ivory hunt and Roman use of the animals in war and circuses—for a thousand years and is greatly diminished in West Africa. These magnificent animals—the larg-

est land mammals on earth—are still to be found in thirty-six African nations, in populations that range from as few as twenty animals to as many as eighty-five thousand.

The dip in the African elephant's back and the position of its head, held slightly lower than the shoulders, are useful in differentiating between the two elephant species. Threatened as never before by ivory poachers, the African elephant's numbers were reduced by at least half between 1980 and 1989, leaving no more than 600,000 animals in the wild.

THE ELEPHANT'S PHYSIQUE

The most obvious difference between the African and the Asian elephant is size. Elephants continue to grow throughout their lives, although the rate slackens in the middle years, so size is often a good clue to an elephant's age. The forest elephants of Africa, adapted to the dense equatorial woodlands, are often smaller than Asian elephants. Asian elephants usually approach an ultimate shoulder height of between 8 and 10 feet (2.5 and 3 m). African bush elephants exhibit considerable sexual dimorphism in terms of size: Males grow up to 14 feet (4 m) at the shoulder, while mature females are usually a little more than half that size. Asian elephants may weigh up to 5 tons (4.5 metric tons), compared with about 3½ tons (3.2 metric tons) for female and up to 6 tons (5.4 metric tons) for male African bush elephants.

The quick check to determine which species you are looking at, if faced with only one elephant or with specimens that are some distance away, would be to examine ear shape. Conveniently, the African elephant's ears are shaped like the African continent, while the Asian elephant's smaller ears resemble India in outline. Looking at the animals' backs is also helpful; Asian elephants' backs are convex, while African elephants' backs look slightly scooped out in the center. Most elephants in Western zoos and circuses are Asian, although the popular image, drawn from Tarzan matinees and wave upon wave of Hollywood safari films, is of a wild-eared African elephant charging through the bush.

Since African and Asian elephants belong to separate genera, they also differ in a host of other small ways. The tusks of the Asian elephant are much less pronounced than those of the African elephant. Female Asian elephants are generally believed to be tuskless, but in fact their tusks are so underdeveloped that they are not visible beyond the lip line. The African elephant's trunk functions with the aid of two finger-like projections at the tip, while the Asian has only one such protuberance. The African elephant has a broad, smooth, gently sloping forehead and stands with its head a little lower than its shoulders. By contrast, the Asian elephant's head, crowned by the double-domed structures at the top of its skull, is the highest point on its body. In more ways than not, though, the two species are quite similar, and they share a remarkable physiognomy and a social structure unlike that of any other animal.

Normally, female elephants become sexually mature at about age eleven or twelve and usually have a first calf a few years later. One reason for the lag is the elephant's unusually long gestation period, which stretches to some twenty-two months, after which time a female usually gives birth following a fairly easy labor. (In fact, researchers say they find it difficult to tell whether a female elephant is pregnant, and are often surprised when a female appears after a few hours away from the

Mother and child, the essential unit of the elephant family: This baby, using its mouth to suckle, is large enough to be nearing the end of its nursing period of about four years.

© Charles G. Summers, Jr./Tom Stack & Associates

herd with a new calf.) A single calf is the norm, but twins are not un-heard of.

Newborn male calves of both species weigh up to 260 pounds (117 kg) and females slightly less, about 200 to 220 pounds (90 to 99 kg). Calves of both sexes are about 4 feet (1.2 m) long and about 2 feet, 9 inches (8.3 m) at the shoulder—a tiny fraction of their mothers' size. Adult elephants do not have very obvious body hair, but new calves often have a lot, particularly around the face and neck. Their ears may at first show tender pink splotches, especially on the backs. These splotches gradually fade to the elephant's usual dark gray or black color.

If all goes well, the baby begins suckling, using its mouth, from its mother's two breasts, which are in about the same position as a woman's breasts, within a few hours of birth. An elephant cannot survive without its mother's milk until it is at least two years old, although recently an acceptable formula has been devised for orphans (see page 72). Youngsters do, however, begin to nibble on vegetation and learn how to drink water when they are a few months old. In many cases, calves continue to nurse until they are four or five years old, or sometimes even older; this is subject, of course, to the mother's tolerance and availability of surplus milk. Many females produce another calf two to three years after a baby's birth, and an older calf's growing tusks can cause the mother quite a lot of pain if she continues to nurse it.

A young elephant is well nurtured by its mother and her female relatives, and learns from them about danger as well as the many necessary skills for survival in a terrain that can sometimes be inhospitable. In fact, the entire social organization of elephants is centered around caring for the calves (see Chapter 3).

One of the first tasks for a young elephant is to begin to master the use of its trunk, a unique organ that extends between the tusks, and is long enough to sweep the ground. The long, tubular trunk—part nose and part upper lip—is controlled by some sixty thousand muscles, a structure that gives the trunk great flexibility as well as the strength to grasp and lift heavy objects. The fingerlike projections at the end of the trunk also give the elephant sufficient dexterity to pick up a pen or even a dime. Gaining command of such a complex organ is a feat that often results in some highly comical moments among the nurslings, who at first find their trunks something of a nuisance.

A primary function of the trunk is breathing, since it contains the nostrils, although an elephant can also breathe through its mouth. As part nose, the trunk is also necessary for olfactory perception. Sense of smell is highly developed in elephants, far more so than their eyesight, and is used to test for a vocabulary of scents in the air, ground, vegetation, and other animals. The trunk, when used in this way, is an indis-

A newborn elephant's trunk is a fairly useless and ungainly appendage. Learning its many uses is an essential part of growing up. Meanwhile, the youngster can depend upon the entire herd to turn their superior size to its protection.

© Stan Osolinski/M.L. Dembinsky Jr. Photography Assoc.

When thirsty, elephants use their trunks to siphon water into their mouths. In hot weather, they also may spray themselves with water to reduce body temperature or go for a cooling swim when water is plentiful.

pensable organ of communication, providing important information about everything from sex to hidden dangers.

Small hairs on the trunk aid the elephant's sense of touch, and elephants frequently fondle members of their own herd and others with their trunks. Sounds produced by forcing air out of the trunk supplement those produced by the vocal chords, giving the elephant what scientists have begun to discover is a fairly complex "language" for communicating with each other (see Chapter 4). The trunk plays a role in producing the familiar high-pitched, angry trumpet, but elephants also talk to each other in rumbles, squeaks, roars, and other distinctive sounds produced in the larynx.

Occasionally, an elephant that is very vexed might strike another creature with its trunk, or use it to hurl some object out of its way. Cynthia Moss, who has studied elephants for many years as director of the Amboseli Elephant Project in Kenya, tells of elephants killing cattle with one quick and powerful thwack of the trunk. Usually, however, the elephant treats its trunk very gently, and observers of elephants have often seen trunks draped over tusks with artful nonchalance.

Such care is necessary, since the trunk is essential to eating and drinking. Adult elephants may consume up to 300 pounds (135 kg) of vegetation each day, although only about 40 percent of this is completely digested; elephants also take in as much as 50 gallons (190 l) of water. With its trunk the elephant can pluck its favorite fruits from trees and gently strip their branches of tender leaves. The trunk also enables the elephant to pull up tremendous quantities of grass by the roots, and assist any youngsters that might be having trouble feeding on their own. Young elephants drink with their mouths until they have deciphered the intricacies of the trunk, but the usual method among adults is to siphon water with their trunks and pour it into their throats.

Without the trunk, this consumption would not be feasible, and neither would be the frequent mud and dust baths, an essential part of elephant hygiene, which protect the animals' tough but delicate skin from the sun, discourage flies, and help it rid itself of parasitic insects. An elephant with an injured trunk is seriously handicapped and, in most cases, will die of starvation.

An elephant's tusks are simply oversize incisor teeth, which people have valued through the ages as ivory, and have used primarily for carvings. Young elephants are born with milk tusks, which never grow longer than a few inches, and are shed after a year or so. Permanent tusks emerge in their place and, in the case of the African elephant, continue to grow throughout life, becoming visible sometime between age two and three.

Male African elephants allowed to live out their long lifespan of approximately seventy years may sport tusks that measure 10 feet (3 m) in length and together weigh more than 440 pounds (200 kg). The heaviest recorded weight—460 pounds (209 kg)—is that of a pair of tusks taken from an elephant at Mount Kilimanjaro near the border between Kenya and Tanzania in 1897; the pair is on display at the British Museum in London. Tusk growth in female African elephants is much less spectacular. Their tusks are far shorter and more slender, and their combined weight often does not exceed 44 pounds (20 kg). With the Asian elephant, only the males grow visible tusks, and these, although they occasionally reach 6 feet (1.8 m) in length, are generally smaller still than those of female African elephants.

The elephant may use its tusks to pull bark off trees, lift heavy objects, dig salt and essential minerals from the earth, and even dig wells, from which other animals drink when the elephants have satisfied their thirst, to bring groundwater to the surface in times of drought. An elephant with an injured trunk can sometimes gather enough food to remain in good condition by using its tusks as a kind of scoop or shovel. If seriously threatened, the elephant can, and will, gore an opponent, but this rarely happens, since elephants have other means of protecting themselves.

The elephant's trunk is a useful adaptation that enables the animal to exploit a nourishing food source that most other animals cannot reach. In the African bush, only the giraffe can partake of browse growing at higher levels.

© Walt Anderson/Visuals Unlimited

Above: The tusks, essentially overgrown teeth used to feed, fight, and manipulate the environment by digging and lifting, are perhaps the most elegant feature of elephant anatomy.

As for their nemeses, elephants are said to dislike rhinoceroses, but usually respond to their presence by moving away. Besides humans, elephants really only display wariness around lions (in Africa) and the much larger tigers of Asia. Among themselves, elephants rarely fight, although males often spar with their tusks and trunks, and push against each other in a show of strength and as a means of establishing dominance. Only when two males in *musth,* a condition of heightened hormonal activity that plays a crucial role in successful competition for breeding females (see page 80), happen to meet does serious tusker-to-tusker combat sometimes ensue. These fights can be to the death, but the less dominant animal also has the choice of walking away from the conflict—and often does.

The tusks are one of an individual elephant's most characteristic features. Some tusks are slim and straight, while others may project at very different angles, curve sharply, cross in front, or even spiral downward toward the cheek, occasionally becoming ingrown and posing a serious health problem. In the course of a lifetime an elephant may break a tusk, but the broken tooth continues growing throughout the elephant's life, and patterns of use may even allow it to catch up with the other tusk in length. Like a right- or left-handed human, elephants often favor one tusk over the other.

Left: Folklore holds that the rhinoceros, runner-up to the elephant among the world's largest land mammals, is the elephant's mortal enemy. In reality, this African elephant and black rhino facing off in the Ngorongoro Crater of Tanzania would rather walk away than fight.

© Fritz Polking/M.L. Dembinsky Jr. Photography Assoc.

A fairly common genetic variation causes some animals to be born with only one tusk or with none, but this is usually not a serious handicap. In India, tusklessness is common enough that such elephants are given a special name, *makhna,* and in some areas as many as 50 percent of male elephants may be affected. Some scientists have speculated that the Asian species may be following a natural evolutionary course toward tusklessness. Others see in such a trend prime evidence of humankind's heavy-handedness in interacting with nature, the inevitable result of our pursuit of ivory, which may have caused wild elephants to select against tusks as a means of ensuring their own survival.

The elephant's foot, which for some reason has been popular with humans for use as rather stubby occasional tables and umbrella stands, is an admirable piece of engineering and the secret of the animal's ability to move with silent agility. Though the sturdy, columnar form of the foot and foreleg suggests otherwise, the elephant actually walks on tiptoe. This may seem impossible if we consider how precarious and exhausting are our own efforts to walk on tiptoe for more than a few minutes. But the difference between a person and an elephant walking on tiptoe is that the elephant's foot is supported by a cushiony wedge of fatty tissue that functions like a giant shock absorber. The fatty material is held in place by the thick skin covering the foot, which leaves enough

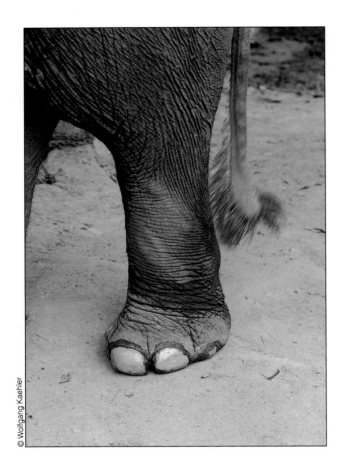

Above: The elephant's foot may look clumsy, but its marvelous "shock absorber" construction gives the animal agility and a sure sense of balance.

room for the tissue to shift in response to the animal's movements. Not only does this shock absorber expand and contract as the elephant withdraws and bears down with its full weight, but it molds itself around the contours of rugged or steep terrain, muffling sound and giving the elephant amazing surefootedness and balance. Despite its agility, the elephant's usual pace is quite leisurely, about 6 miles (10 km) per hour, although it can walk for long distances at about 15 miles (24 km) per hour when necessary. Speeds higher than that are difficult, and charges, usually at about 18 miles (29 km) per hour, are brief because the animal quickly becomes exhausted.

The elephant's skin, particularly that of its large, intricately veined ears, is a fine adaptation to the animal's size and the extreme climates in which it lives. The elephant has developed a very thick skin, which helps hold heat in its massive body and prevents any precipitous drops in body temperature. (The elephant would have a difficult time adjusting to such drops due to its slow metabolism.) In most of their range, however, both African and Asian elephants face a different problem: how to get rid of excess heat generated in a sun-filled tropical habitat.

The ear, with its multiplicity of blood vessels within a much thinner skin, solves this problem for the elephant very nicely. Blood passes through the ear close to the skin's surface, allowing heat—as much as 16 degrees Fahrenheit (9°C), probably the largest fluctuation in body temperature ever noted in a healthy mammal—to be dispelled into the air. By flapping and fanning its ears, the elephant gives the evaporation and cooling process a further assist.

This release of heat is especially important since elephants lack sweat glands, the usual mechanisms that help mammals cool down quickly. In lieu of sweat, the elephant tries to remain cool by seeking shade during

Right: The elephant's ear, constructed from thinner skin than that covering the rest of its body, is crisscrossed by a fine network of blood vessels that release excess body heat directly into the air, allowing the creatures to withstand the extreme temperatures prevalent in parts of Africa and Asia.

the hottest part of the day, and by bathing when sufficient water is available (elephants are strong swimmers, and appear greatly to enjoy playing in water).

Although most scientists doubt that large ear size plays much of a role in the elephant's acute hearing, the fanlike outer ears have an important communications function. Like many other animals, the elephant prefers to negotiate rather than fight when faced with trouble. One way in which the animal can do this is by making itself appear larger through behavior known as a threat display. Just as some birds puff up their feathers or toads inflate their body cavities when threatened by predators, the elephant follows a similar instinct when it stops in its tracks before a potential enemy and spreads its ears as wide as possible. This makes the elephant's head, and by implication its body, appear much larger than it actually is; in the case of the African elephant, a full ear extension at least triples its head size. In addition, the dark, smooth surface of the ears forms a perfect backdrop for the elephant's gleaming white tusks, making these potential weapons appear especially formidable. Frequently, such a display is enough to make a threatening animal back down, and renders an exhausting charge or use of the tusks unnecessary.

Elephants are legendary, of course, for their long memories. The Greek philosopher and scientist Aristotle, who dissected an elephant during the fourth century B.C., was probably the first person to probe

This African matriarch, frozen in a listening position with her ears held wide, can easily move into a charge should she deem it necessary to ward off a potential enemy. Among smaller animals, the threatening elephant's size alone—augmented by the extended ears—is usually sufficient warning.

seriously the question of the elephant's intelligence. Modern scientists have performed only a few behavioral experiments involving memory with elephants, and these tests indicate that the animals recall complex forms of information after as long as eight years.

The structure and development of the elephant's brain, not dissimilar from a human's, also lends credence to its reputation for intelligence. The brain of an adult male African elephant weighs as much as 11.9 pounds (5.4 kg), four times as much as a grown man's brain and more than that of any other land mammal. However, brain size per se is not the prime indicator of intelligence, and animals with proportionally smaller brains, such as the orangutan, may be nearly as intelligent as the elephant. A better guide to intelligence levels is probably the degree to which an animal's brain develops after birth. Here the elephant compares favorably with humans. An elephant calf's brain weighs about 26 percent of its adult weight, while a human baby's weighs about 35 percent. For most mammals, the corresponding figure would be about 90 percent. Both baby humans and baby elephants make up the difference between the birth and adult weight of their brains during their long childhood and adolescence, a period when intensive learning and corresponding brain development takes place.

ELEPHANTS AND THEIR ENVIRONMENT

Elephants of all ages and both sexes spend most of their day eating. Grazing and foraging take up about sixteen hours of each day and sleep only about four. The elephant's sleeping hours are split between periods of standing rest throughout the day and a briefer time, usually toward daybreak, when the animals might lie down. The remaining hours, scientists say, are spent in travel. Periods of elephant activity follow a typical pattern with peaks of movement in search of food and water in the early hours of morning, at late afternoon, and again around midnight— a serene and harmonious pattern.

Although it is difficult to know precisely, scientists speculate that elephants may once have migrated over vast territories. Most likely these primeval herds acted on a large store of knowledge accumulated and passed on through many generations as the animals went about their peaceful quest for forage and water in rainy and dry seasons. Today's herds, forced into the diminished and isolated territories that humans allot them, can only follow their traditional behavior patterns to a limited degree. We may know that a certain group of African elephants confined to a semiarid habitat has a wet season home range of about 3,750 kilometers (2,250 mi.) and that others, confined to a lusher but much more densely populated area, tend to stay put within a more mod-

© Gerry Ellis/The Wildlife Collection

est range of 14 to 52 kilometers (8.4 to 31.2 mi.). We may also know that an African elephant travels, on average, about 14 to 52 kilometers (7.2 mi.) in a twenty-four-hour period and an Asian elephant, with less habitat available, only between 1 and 8.5 kilometers (.6 and 5.1 mi.). But these figures tell us nothing of elephant lives in the thousands of years before humankind's exploding population altered forever the range and meaning of wilderness on every continent.

Because their intelligence, body size, and dexterous trunks enable them to alter their surroundings substantially, elephants probably always have had a tremendous impact upon their habitat. In addition to shaping the environment to suit themselves, elephants bring about changes that also affect other animal species. One example is the dry-season digging of ''wells'' by the desert elephants of Namibia. When an extreme drought coupled with poaching killed off most of these elephants in the 1980s, their wells went unexcavated, to the detriment of other animals in the area that have inadequate memories and capabilities for finding hidden water on their own. Elephants have also been observed

Elephants felling trees and trampling brush with their gigantic bodies clear the way for new growth of shrubs, bushes, and grasses—essential foods for zebra, wildebeest, rhinoceros, and many species of antelope.

building dams, again with positive consequences for animals of many species.

Another example of elephants altering their environment, and one that causes conservationists to lose a lot of sleep, is the activity of tree-felling, which has been studied most closely in Africa. Under dry-season conditions, elephants increase their intake of *browse* (leaves and shoots of bushes and trees), which contains more protein than the dried-out grasses that may be more plentiful at that time of year. As the dry season wears on, elephants may begin pushing over trees in order to obtain browse beyond the trunk's reach. But sometimes elephants bulldoze trees, particularly slow-growing acacias, for no apparent reason. They also strip the bark from baobab trees with their tusks; the animals sometimes eat part of the spongy interior of the trunk, but in many cases, they simply strip the trees and leave them unprotected against insects and disease.

Tree-felling worries conservationists because sometimes the lost tree species appear not to grow again, at least not during many observation periods. This lack of tree replacement not only may cause soil erosion, but also may be problematic for giraffes, who dine mostly from treetops. On the other hand, tree-felling encourages coppage growth from the trees' roots, which creates browse that is within cropping range of shorter animals. It also clears the way for new, more nutritious grass-lands that provide food for zebras, wildebeests, and scores of other grazing animals. Without intensive, long-term study, there is simply no way for us to know definitively if the elephant's seemingly destructive activities are a vital link in the endless cycle of regeneration of plains, bush, and forest, or whether the elephant, experiencing an unnatural squeeze from humans, is systematically destroying not only its habitat but that of other creatures.

The unique role the elephant plays in helping to disperse and germinate the seeds of several species of plants suggests that the animal's behaviors may be essential, that they (and perhaps the elephant's very physiognomy) may in fact have evolved to solve some of a harsh environment's special problems. The elephant's dung, containing much partially digested material, is particularly rich in nutrients vital to germinating seeds, which may be lacking in certain poor soils of Africa. Studies have shown that the seeds of certain trees may not germinate without first passing through the elephant's digestive system; the seeds also receive a boost from the accompanying natural fertilizer. One such tree is the doum palm, whose seed (the source of vegetable ivory) and leathery pith is so hard that only baboons are able to crack and eat it. Likewise, only an elephant's powerful digestive juices seem to be able to liberate the seed from the stubborn pith so that a new life can begin.

Elephants often destroy large stands of acacia trees, an essential food of the giraffe, but studies show that the animals are a prime link in the dispersion and successful germination of acacia seeds.

Other seeds (including those of the acacia that troubles conservationists so) germinate in much higher percentages when their hard seed coatings have been presoftened by the elephant's digestive juices. Such seeds are ready to germinate as soon as rain finds them, and do not have to undergo the lengthy process of weathering and softening by the elements. Studies of the Ivory Coast's Tai Forest suggest that the seeds of twenty-one of seventy-one tropical tree species there are chiefly dispersed by elephants. Without the elephant, would scores of other animal species perish because the foods necessary to their survival simply refused to grow? Would much of the African savannah become a wizened desert? Fossil evidence supports the view that megafaunal extinctions in Central and South America during the last ice age led to wholesale extinctions of other species, both plant and animal. Clearly, the more scientists learn, the more troubling such questions—at present unanswerable—become.

Humanity clearly has much to learn from elephants—both about the two remaining species themselves and about the way these animals influence and enrich their environment. Although ethological and environmental research did not begin in earnest until the early 1960s, we have almost thirty years of data derived from observing several wild African elephant populations. Ironically, just as we have accumulated a solid base of information from which to begin trying to understand these complex, long-lived mammals and the ways they may be necessary to the survival of other creatures in their environment, the more numerous African elephant is threatened with extinction, and likewise, the Asian elephant hangs on tenaciously, albeit from an extremely slender thread. The events of the next decade will probably determine whether these animals will be with us in the next century in sufficient numbers for us to learn from, admire, and enjoy.

Above: African elephants often exhibit a voracious appetite for the bark of certain trees, particularly the baobab. Although the bark most likely provides the elephants with vitamins and minerals otherwise missing from their diet, stripped trees are vulnerable to insects and disease and eventually die.

Below: A Zambian elephant has broken its tusk in the crook of this tree in the Luangwa Valley. As human populations hunger for more farmland and squeeze elephants into ever smaller areas, scientists must determine whether the animals' destruction of trees and other plants contributes to permanent degradation of the environment or simply remains part of an ageless cycle of renewal that predates human demands upon the land.

The African Elephant: Poaching and the Road to Extinction

With 600,000 African elephants left in the wild, how close is the species, *really*, to extinction? If poaching continues in the 1990s at the rate observed throughout the 1980s— some 10 percent of the total population each year—few if any African elephants will be left to greet the twenty-first century. The elephant's usual birth rate, about 3 or 4 percent per annum, is simply insufficient to make up such devastating losses.

The road to extinction is more complicated than a straight numbers game, however. Ivory poaching brings to the African elephant's decline a number of twists and turns that serve to compound the problems of a simple reduction of numbers. One of these is the problem of a limited gene pool, the effects of which have already been observed in such threatened species as the giant panda. When a large population of animals becomes fragmented through a disaster, some small groups may inevitably be cut off from contact with other members of their species. Michael Schmidt, a veterinarian at the Washington Park Zoo in Portland,

Oregon, concerned with captive breeding programs, suggests that at a certain size, say five hundred animals, isolated groups of Asian elephants lack the genetic diversity to survive. The animals in such a group may continue to breed, but without periodic infusions of new genetic material, the offspring they produce will be less and less viable. Localized extinction eventually may take place without any further interference from humans.

Poaching also disrupts the complex elephant social structure in a number of subtle ways that may reduce the African species' already modest breeding rate. Since elephants' tusks continue to grow throughout their long lives, mature musth bulls sport the most impressive ivory and therefore are most attractive to poachers. These are precisely the same animals that mature female elephants—those most likely to raise offspring to maturity— prefer and encourage as mates. Without musth males available, female elephants do not necessarily stop mating. Says Cynthia Moss, "They adjust, but the reproductive rate probably slows down for a while. There are a number of reasons why the rate would go down. The younger males may not have as high a sperm count as the musth males, and also the young ones may be inept. The actual physical knowledge of how to mate isn't there."

Moss continues, "If there isn't one single dominant male who can guard the female, there's probably a lot of stress as she gets chased by a lot of males who may be around the same age. Under those circumstances, she may not conceive." The absence of musth males may have negative consequences for selection as well. "If you've got twenty males in a population and they're all around the same age," Moss says, "then they may be passing on genes that wouldn't have been passed on at all in a population in which the males

In the 1970s and 1980s, African elephants joined the list of highly endangered species that includes spotted cats such as the cheetah. The culprits: poachers in search of the elephant's highly valued ivory tusks.

© Dr. John Cunningham/Visuals Unlimited

©Gerry Ellis/The Wildlife Collection

were allowed to get older and the secondary sexual characteristics [size, strength] were what made them successful.''

In many East African elephant populations, males thirty-five years old and over have been killed, then the poachers moved on to the younger males and older females for their ivory even though their tusks are ludicrously tiny compared to the giant tusks of the vanquished musth males. Scientists have noted with horror that in some areas, elephant families consist mainly of frightened, confused juveniles and have no sense of clear leadership. The loss of the matriarchs has further disrupted the African elephant's social order in ways that affect reproduction and survival. ''In Amboseli,'' Moss points out, ''the family is often disrupted for a couple of years when a big matriarch dies. Not only will reproductive rates be lowered, but many calves may die'' before the family's equilibrium is restored. Without the matriarchs and their wisdom—or indeed, many of the females who ordinarily would have been in line to succeed them— such equilibrium becomes an ever more distant prospect.

African musth bulls bearing tusks ten feet (3 m) in length and more were once a common sight in the wild. Now the mature male elephants that bear such massive ivory have been all but wiped out, leaving only young bulls, which are less favored by breeding females as mates.

© Rosenthal Art Slides

chapter two

ELEPHANTS IN HISTORY

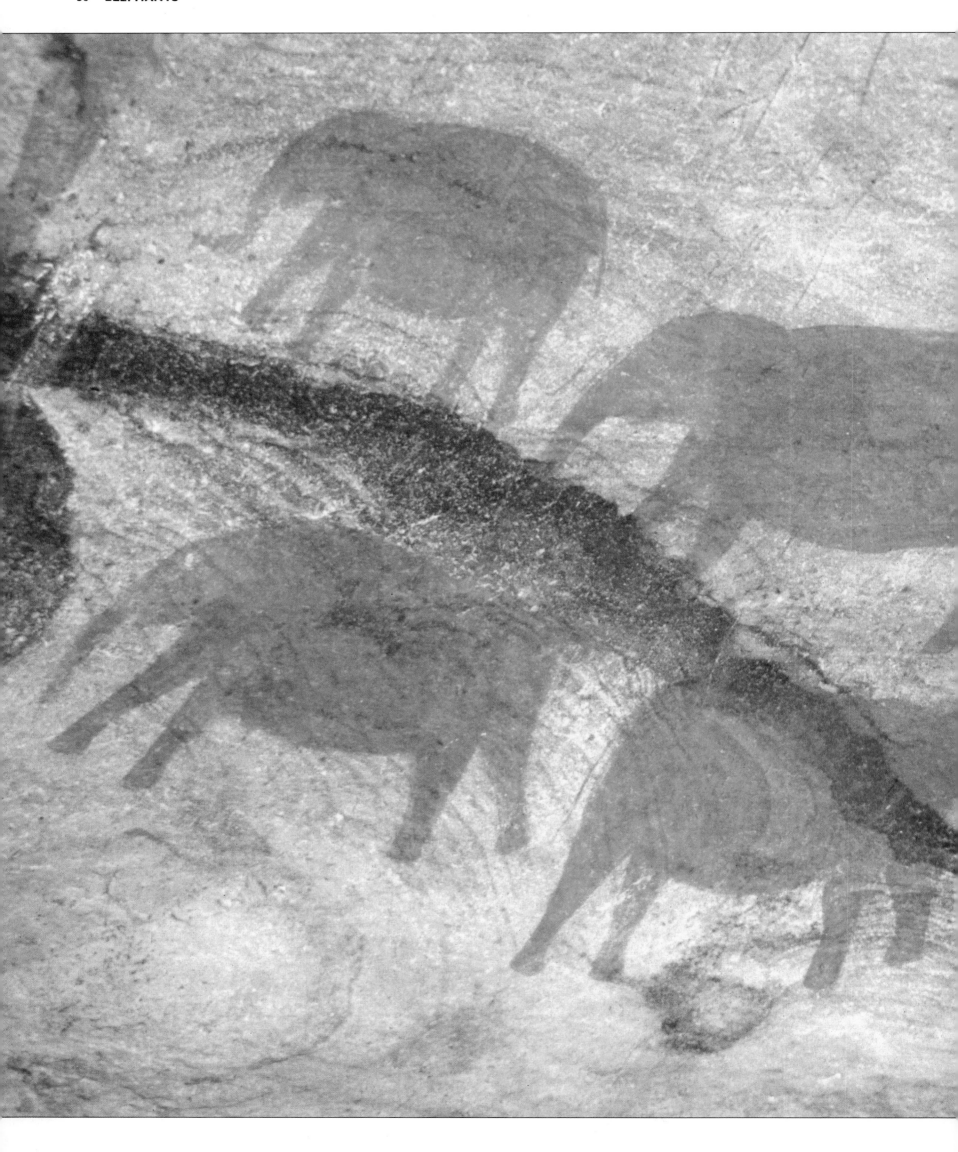

The sage told a pilgrim that the earth rests on the backs of four elephants who stand upon a tortoise. When asked what the tortoise stood upon, the sage declared that it stood upon another elephant.

"And what does the elephant stand upon?" the pilgrim asked. "Oh," the sage replied, "it's elephants and tortoises all the way down."

Indian myth, quoted in To Whom It May Concern: An Investigation of the Art of Elephants *by David Gucwa and James Ehmann*

Humanity's first association with the elephant undoubtedly was as its hunter. The elephant's yield of great quantities of meat; large, tough skin; bones; and ivory would have been useful in meeting many of early humans' primary needs for shelter and implements. A pit discovered in present-day Czechoslovakia containing about nine hundred mammoth skeletons and numerous prehistoric hunters' tools is one of the best pieces of evidence that man hunted these early elephants fairly intensively. Man also may have pursued the more primitive mastodon, which was contemporary with the mammoth.

As an object of the hunt, the elephant figures prominently in humans' earliest artistic efforts. Neolithic rock paintings found across the length and breadth of Africa depict elephants in surprising detail. Anthropologists theorize that such paintings could have played a magical role in the lives of their creators, who may have believed (much like tribal peoples today who fear that by being photographed they will give a stranger

Opposite page: The elephant is a central figure in scores of prehistoric rock paintings, such as this Bushman creation, which can be found scattered across Africa.

power over their souls) that producing such pictures would give the hunter power over his prey. Whatever their function, such paintings are plentiful and well preserved, valuable clues to human beings' emergence as image-makers.

The elephant's tusks, or ivory, have also figured in human artistic expression for thousands of years. A discussion of the role of ivory in the world's history follows on pages 92–96. But whether carved from ivory or depicted in other media, the image of the elephant continued to be a favorite subject of artists in cultures as diverse as those of pre-dynastic Egypt and China, quite likely as a result of the increasing complexity of the animal's relationship with civilization.

ELEPHANTS AS WORKERS

The precise moment when the elephant became more to humans than a convenient source of meat and raw materials is impossible to pinpoint. Probably the crucial shift occurred about ten thousand years ago, an-thropologists suggest, when agriculture began to be practiced on a larger scale and with an efficiency that supplanted hunting and gather-ing as humans' primary livelihood. Somewhere along the way—or, more likely, many times in many widely separated spots—as men and women tilled the ground and began to build permanent settlements, the notion that the elephant's strength and intelligence might be of more value to them than its meat and ivory began to gain currency.

The first early experiments in domesticating the elephant probably took place in Southeast Asia, perhaps with young animals orphaned when their mothers were killed in the hunt. Very quickly the animals proved their worth in a variety of tasks, particularly in moving heavy logs such as teak in order to clear the densely forested mountain slopes of the region for farming. As men became more experienced with the elephants, they developed a method of training them that built upon their natural gregariousness, intelligence, and need to trust instilled from the young elephants' earliest days in the matriarchal herd. This method, little changed over the ages, survives intact today in the few remaining elephant work and training camps in India, Nepal, Thailand, and Myanmar.

Ideally, each young elephant in training is paired with a boy or young man of about the same age as the animal who will serve as its trainer. (In India, such a trainer is called a *mahout,* in Myanmar he is known as an *oozie,* and in Nepal he is referred to as a *phanti.*) Since both man and elephant live to about age seventy, the hope is that the two will develop an intimate and trusting relationship that will last throughout their productive lives. Training can begin at around age five, but ele-

Men carved objects from mammoth ivory as early as twenty thousand years ago. The craft also has ancient roots in Egypt, where ornaments carved from elephant ivory some six thousand years ago have been found. This Egyptian plaque dates from the eleventh or twelfth century B.C.

phants are not normally put to work until they have reached adulthood—about age twenty; training the growing animal earlier would be harmful to its health. Because of this, most work camps prefer to capture and train wild animals that are only a few years away from working age to save the expense of feeding and caring for the animals and their mahouts during the two decades when they are unproductive. Another reason why young work elephants must be captured is simply a matter of demographics: In the past the demand for work animals could be quite high, with some camps housing as many as three thousand elephants; since birth rates in captivity tend to be much lower than in the wild, capturing wild animals is the only way to supply the demand for them.

The use of elephants as work animals is a venerable tradition practiced throughout most of southern Asia, and whose origins are shrouded in prehistory.

The method of capturing work elephants has changed little over the centuries. As shown here, the wild animals enter the *keddah*, a corral built along one of the herd's regular paths, and a gate is lowered behind them. The *mahouts* can then select the young elephants they wish to train.

Capture usually involves building a large corral, or *keddah,* in the forest at the end of an elephant trail leading to a source of water. The mahouts wait for an elephant herd to take the path, and when the animals are safely inside the keddah, a hidden gate is quickly lowered. At this stage, the mahouts depend heavily upon their already-tamed elephants to accomplish the task of separating out the animals of appropriate age and condition for training. A wild elephant will allow a mahout and an assistant on elephantback to ride up close; at this point, an assistant drops to the ground and quickly slips a noose around the wild elephant's back leg. The mahout, with the help of his mount, then leads his wild charge, by now struggling fiercely, to a nearby tree where he will be tethered for the next few days. When all the appropriate animals have been secured, the gate is raised, and the free members of the herd depart the chaotic scene.

With their voracious appetites, the captive elephants grow ravenous with hunger within a few hours. The mahouts exploit the captives' hunger during the coming days, using the task of providing food and water to begin building the initial bonds of trust with their new charges. When the wild elephants begin to rage less forcefully against their loss of freedom, the mahouts enlist the tame elephants once again to help escort the new animals back to camp.

Training is accomplished through a combination of negative and positive reinforcement, ideally with the emphasis on the latter. The mahout may at first rely heavily on a *hawkus,* a sharp, hooked instrument, to control his elephant which, of course, is many times larger than he is and probably still very unhappy about being captured. When the elephant behaves threateningly, the mahout uses the hawkus to prick the animal's sensitive trunk. After a number of repetitions, the fear evoked by the painful jab usually causes the elephant to stand quietly; eventually, just the sight of the hawkus will have the same effect.

Once the elephant responds appropriately to the *hawkus,* the more positive aspects of training are introduced. One way in which the mahout establishes a bond with his elephant is through grooming him; daily baths and mudpacks for the animal are part of the training routine. This is a pleasant activity for elephants in the wild, so the mahout enhances the experience by talking soothingly to the elephant and lavishing it with attention when grooming it. As training begins in earnest, special foods such as bananas or rice balls may be offered as a reward when the elephant performs a specific behavior, such as lifting a foot upon the mahout's verbal command.

It is considered a major breakthrough when the elephant has successfully been trained to accept a rider. This is usually accomplished in a single marathon session that may take anywhere from a few hours to a full day and night. First, the elephant is led into a special enclosure equipped with a pulleylike apparatus. This apparatus is used to haul the mahout high into the air and then lower him onto the back of the elephant's neck. This is an alien experience for the elephant, and like a horse in the same position, it usually tries to throw the mahout off. Repeating the procedure many times—the mahout hauled safely out of the elephant's range whenever the young animal becomes violent— eventually convinces the elephant to keep still and allow this strange new behavior.

The elephant has not yet been broken, however, until it has been trained to sit so that the mahout can mount and dismount. For this stage of the training, the pulley is used to lower a very heavy padded wood block onto the young elephant's back. Once again, the animal usually struggles against this new experience. The weight of the wood wins out before too long, however, and the pressure causes the elephant to assume the first desired position: sitting on its haunches with its forelegs stretched out in front. When the wood block is lifted from the elephant's back, the animal struggles to its feet—the second position the mahout wants the animal to take. Next, verbal commands are introduced with the lowering and raising of the wood block, and soon the mahout, comfortably ensconced on his elephant's neck, can simply rest his hand on the animal's back and shout *"Hmit!"* and the elephant will sit. Once the mahout has dismounted, the verbal command *"Tah!"* is all that is needed to induce the elephant to stand. The animal is now ready to begin learning the more specialized skills needed to transport and control logs. As part of this phase of the training, the elephant learns some sixty verbal commands as well as corresponding touch commands in which the mahout may use his foot, hand, or the blunt end of the hawkus to signal to the animal.

© Wolfgang Kaehler

The elephant's natural love of water facilitates bonding and the growth of trust between *mahout* and trainee during regular bathtimes.

Although elephants are sometimes given light packs of a few hundred pounds to transport, their weak shoulders keep them from being very efficient pack animals. Great care also must be taken to protect the animals' high-ridged backbones. They are far more useful in logging operations, today a prime source of foreign exchange earnings for Southeast Asian countries. The elephants easily move the dead weight of trees and bring them to nearby rivers for transport.

Not surprisingly, elephants contribute to the smooth working of the logging operations with their intelligence as well as their strength. They quickly grasp the purpose of their work, and if, for instance, a log jam develops, they are perfectly capable of solving the problem without the assistance of the mahout. Even considering the traditional 162-day elephant work year (three days on, two days off, with three months off during the hottest part of the year), developed as the best way of keeping the animals happy and in good condition, elephants are highly efficient workers, far more so than the bulldozers that will one day replace them. An elephant doesn't burn costly fossil fuel or pollute the air; its food is free, and its working life—thirty to thirty-five years—is several times longer than what might be expected of a bulldozer. The elephant also is perfectly suited to the mountainous forest, its natural habitat in Asia—a rugged terrain a bulldozer often has trouble negotiating; and finally, it possesses a problem-solving ability no bulldozer can supply.

Common elephant lore has it that only Asian elephants are trainable. This is not true, as a training program established in 1899 by King

Work elephants are particularly useful in logging operations. In the hardwood forests that are an important source of foreign currency for Southeast Asian nations such as Thailand, they operate more efficiently and with far more intelligence than expensive man-made machinery. Ironically, as they provide this valuable service, Asian work elephants help to destroy yet more of their own dwindling habitat.

© Ron Sanford

Left: Elephant rides provide an intimate encounter with the bush and are a popular offering at many Indian game reserves and at Tiger Tops, shown here, in Nepal. As conservationists, governments, and tour operators in Africa look for ways to make the elephant a valuable commodity to the local people, thereby enlisting them in the fight against poaching, elephant rides may also become common in African parks.

Leopold of Belgium in his African colony, now the nation of Zaire, at a town called Kiravunga, proved. Leopold imported Indian mahouts to train local Africans in their techniques, which were successfully used with the small forest elephants native to the region. A second training station opened in 1930 at Gangala na Bodio, near Zaire's Garamba National Park. A few elephants and their *moniteurs* (as *mahouts* are called in this French-speaking country), who once sallied forth to fell trees and clear ground for local residents at a reasonable fee, linger on at this second camp, the aging participants in an experiment that, oddly, never caught on. Occasionally, talk surfaces about the possibility of reviving the program and using the animals to transport tourists around Garamba in the fashion of some Indian and Nepalese game reserves. Soon, an enterprising safari operator will even begin using the larger bush elephants to transport a few visitors around Botswanan game parks.

The diminutive Zairean forest elephants used in the Zairean training experiments, smaller even than their Asian cousins, may indeed be more tractable than the larger African bush elephant, whose habitat is more exposed. Their easy domestication in the last century is less surprising, however, considering that African elephants were used in battle with great success more than two thousand years ago.

ELEPHANTS IN WAR

As humans mastered agriculture, their lives and civilizations quickly grew more complex in every way. Once elephants had been trained to perform a variety of civilian tasks, only a short leap was required to envision the animals' potential usefulness on the battlefield. Although we don't know exactly when elephants were first used in this way, historians agree that the practice originated in Asia.

Below: This German print from the fifteenth century A.D. depicts an elephant in battle and possibly provides a clue to the ancient source of a popular name sometimes given to English public houses, the "Elephant and Castle." The print's fanciful portrayal of the elephant's anatomy also reveals just how unfamiliar Europeans were with such creatures at the time.

Like the tanks used in modern-day warfare, an elephant in full battle regalia must have been a fearsome sight. Most were protected with some sort of armor, whether a garment of heavy leather, facial armor, or even chain mail, and sometimes spears were strapped to their tusks. Tall wooden castles, similar to the *howdah*s (high, usually canopied saddles) used in Asia to seat passengers on elephantback, added considerable height to the elephant's forbidding bulk. Bells hung from the elephants' necks also added to the confusion and noise of battle, which must have included the elephant's own strident vocalizations. A military equivalent of the mahout controlled the elephant from his seat at the base of the animal's neck, and several fighting men concealed inside the castle used

The elephant was an important feature of warfare in Rome and other ancient kingdoms. Although the elephant's strength and size were sometimes augmented with armor and weaponry, the animal's chief role in battle was to trample the enemy and spread confusion.

their advantageous height to rain arrows and toss surprise weapons such as melted pitch into the midst of the enemy forces.

Also like the tank, the elephant was most useful as an advance guard that could wreak destruction and sow panic (particularly among peoples unused to such creatures) before the regular troops marched in. A tank, however, is undoubtedly more dependable, since strategies involving elephants often backfired on their instigators. Once an enemy general became familiar with elephants and understood their tendency to flee pain, the most obvious counterstrategy was to try and create panic among the elephants themselves. If successful, this strategy caused the animals to trample more men on their own side than enemy soldiers.

The age in which elephants were an essential part of warfare lasted from about 500 B.C., when the Assyrian queen Semiramis, lacking elephants of her own, tried to replicate their effect in battle by using elephant dummies in combination with camels, until about A.D. 400, when Roman military might commenced its final decline. (As late as 1844, however, the Thai ruler Rama III led a force that included elephants against a Vietnamese army.) The original fighting elephants had been members of the Asian species, but the demand for the animals in the Middle East and Mediterranean caused military leaders to look for them closer to home. The Ptolemies of Egypt were already partners in an ivory trade with present-day Ethiopia, Eritrea, and Sudan, and it was a fairly easy matter to begin importing the animals for training in warfare. The Carthaginians later sought elephants in North Africa for use in their own campaigns. In both cases, these African war elephants were probably members of the forest race, since contemporary accounts frequently refer to the Asian elephants' greater size and corresponding superiority in battle. From artifacts such as coins, which often confuse the physical attributes of Asian and African elephants, it seems clear that elephant troops during this period rarely must have been composed of purely one species. Conquest, trade, and gifts from friendly or subject rulers of distant lands ensured that elephants of both species found their way into battle side by side.

Alexander the Great was one military leader who successfully turned enemy elephants against their own troops. When Alexander and his Greeks met up with the Punjabi king Porus in the Battle of the Jhelum River in 326 B.C., he had perhaps fifty or sixty elephants to his opponent's more than two hundred. When Porus gained control of an important bridge, effectively trapping Alexander across the river while reinforcements from the Rajah of Kashmir hurried toward them, the Greek general knew he had to act quickly or all would be lost. Under cover of night, he hustled his men and elephants across a more distant bridge, crept up on Porus, and surrounded the Punjabi elephants. Alexander ordered some of his men to concentrate on wounding the elephants, and the confusion created by this enabled Alexander to defeat Porus's infantry—with great losses under elephant foot on both sides.

The campaign involving elephants that has lingered most vividly in human imagination and memory is probably the Carthaginian general Hannibal's challenge to Rome in 218 B.C. at the beginning of the Second Punic War. Hannibal left North Africa with an infantry of fifteen thousand men and fifty-eight elephants, and followed a route that took him through Spain, where he left twenty-one of the elephants with another general. Hannibal continued with only thirty-seven elephants, crossed the Pyrenees, and came to his first major obstacle, the swift-flowing and chilly Rhône River in northeastern France. Various accounts disagree on how the Carthaginians made the crossing, but the elephants most likely accomplished this leg of the journey, their numbers intact,

An illustration accompanying a Thai manuscript describing the qualities of various kinds of elephants dates from the reign of King Rama III in the nineteenth century.

The most famous battle involving elephants occurred in 218 B.C. and pitted forces led by the Carthaginian general Hannibal against the Roman army of Scipio at Trebia. Hannibal and his elephants, shown here crossing the Rhône River, won the battle but lost the war.

with the assistance of rafts. The Alps presented a still more formidable problem, but Hannibal's forces pressed on through cold, deprivation, and ignorance of the rugged terrain. By the time they reached Italy, some men and elephants had perished, although the precise numbers of each remaining are not known.

Still, Hannibal's remaining elephants had the hoped-for effect when his Carthaginians met Roman troops at Trebia and defeated their hated rulers. Soon afterward, though, Hannibal had to put aside his dream of marching on Rome. His men and elephants had marched and fought bravely, but the rigors of their long journey were taking their toll, and both began to die in large numbers. By the time Hannibal called the campaign off, a single elephant—his own mount—was all that remained of his original force of thirty-seven.

ELEPHANTS AS ENTERTAINERS

As elephants became more widely known throughout the ancient world, the Romans came to prize them not as agents of war, like the Greeks and Carthaginians, but chiefly as spectacular animals they could deploy in the Circus Maximus and train for other entertainments. Although some Indian princes apparently liked to pit elephants against each other in fights, the Romans indulged their taste for such contests on a far larger scale. Details of the ancient Roman concerns that made it their business to scour Africa for wild animals are few, although Ostia was a center for receiving animals shipped from Leptis Magna, a Tripolitanian city, or from intermediate stations in Sicily.

The numbers of animals imported, too, are hard to come by, but they must have been large, for the Romans were very fond of animal fights. In a single day of the games organized by the ruler Pompey in 55 B.C., more than six hundred lions perished. And elephants, while they took up more room in stabling than cats, were much in demand for fights against lions, bulls, rhinoceroses, men on foot, men on horseback, and, of course, each other. Elephants, with their obvious intelligence and other sensitive qualities, must have been one of the few animals to gain the Roman crowds' respect and pity. In the same ostentatious Pompeiian games that doomed so many lions, the crowd is said to have demanded mercy for eighteen elephants who, trumpeting in distress after two of their companions fell to men armed with javelins, tried to break through the barrier separating them from the crowd.

The Roman love for animal entertainments had a more benign side. A few animals seem to have been kept simply for display purposes, but trainers soon discovered that elephants could learn to perform elaborate acts such as dance routines, and even seemed to have a real feeling for music. Tightrope performances were also popular, for the elephant, with its uniquely padded foot, was well suited to such displays of agility. The elephants were even persuaded to participate in a sort of drama.

The rhetorician Aelian described an immensely popular act, staged in about A.D. 12, in which several elephant "couples," dressed appropriately, were led to chaises before which a formal banquet had been spread. Reclining before the feast and using their trunks to sample the dainties, the elephants dined in an effective parody of their human audi-

Northwind Picture Archives

Although less common than Roman animal fights, princes of the ancient Indian kingdoms often staged elephant fights. This one, staged in Baroda, took place before European guests.

A tuskless Jumbo amuses visitors to the London Zoo. Fears for public safety led to the animal's purchase by Phineas T. Barnum and subsequent move to America to become a member of the "Greatest Show on Earth"—an emigration that aroused a storm of protest from the British.

ence. The elephants got the last word on the fun, however, when they began spraying each other with water in typical elephantine fashion.

Indeed, the elephant, who in the wild needs no prompting at all to enjoy a frolic in the grass, seems to have had an instinctive grasp of the role of court jester. Another good example of this is a popular anecdote of the time, related by the poet Martial, which told how an elephant pitted against a bull knelt spontaneously before the emperor after dispatching its opponent.

With the decline of Rome, such spectacles subsided, although not before the forest elephant (*Loxodonta africana cyclotis,* the African subspecies native to the area) had been all but destroyed in North Africa. Kings and wealthy individuals continued to keep elephants as specimens in private collections, and occasionally gave them as gifts. Harūn ar-Rashīd gave Charlemagne an African elephant in A.D. 797. Louis IX of France also presented an African elephant to Henry III of England in 1254; the animal was installed in the royal menagerie housed at that time in the Tower of London. Private collectors also sought rare and unusual animal and plant specimens throughout the era of European colonialism, but not until the nineteenth century did the idea of the public zoological garden really take hold. It was at about this time that entrepreneurs such as Phineas T. Barnum revived the idea of the Roman circus, minus the fights, on a grand scale. Suddenly, live elephants, not just their ivory, were in demand again to supply the zoos and circuses of Europe and America.

The most famous captive elephant of this period is probably Jumbo, an African elephant whose name for a long time dominated the popular conception of the elephant and its nature. Jumbo was a main attraction of the London Zoo, which acquired him as a youngster from the Parisian Jardins des Plantes in 1865 in exchange for a rhinoceros. For years Jumbo obediently gave rides to zoo visitors, but at about age twenty, he began to grow restless and unpredictable; he attacked his quarters and, in the end, broke off both tusks. Musth and teething pain have been suggested as the cause of Jumbo's bad humor, although we now know that African bulls do not experience musth until they are at least thirty years of age.

Whatever the cause, Jumbo's behavior served to reinforce the African elephant's reputation as being difficult and untamable. Zoo officials debated what was to be done, for they did not want Jumbo to injure zoo patrons. P. T. Barnum ended the debate when he stepped forward with an offer to buy Jumbo, intending him to lead the procession of smaller Asian elephants in his "Greatest Show on Earth." After several false starts (the British were outraged by this cheeky American theft of *their* elephant, and said so in town hall meetings and a flood of letters to the editors of newspapers all over the country), Jumbo set sail for the United States in 1882. Jumbo never attained in America the fame he had commanded in Britain, for he died shortly after arrival, in 1885, when he was struck by a railway engine in St. Thomas, Ontario, while being marched to his quarters on the circus train. Today, Jumbo's skeleton resides in the Museum of Natural History in New York City.

If Jumbo's fate was unhappy, the fate of other elephants who somehow found themselves in America was sometimes unhappier. Rural Americans, in many cases unsophisticated about the world and frequently devoted to strict, fundamentalist versions of Christianity, did not always react to the gigantic visitors from Africa and Asia with delight. Instead, when fairs and circuses came to town, they brought with them a string of curiosities and some entertainments that many people felt were inspired by the devil. Consequently, the emotion these people often felt toward these strange creatures was a senseless rage and loathing usually reserved for hated fellow humans. One such encounter occurred in a small town in Connecticut in 1824. Some local citizens shot

By the time he arrived in the United States, Jumbo's tusks, broken in a rampage against his own quarters in the London Zoo, would have begun to grow again.

© Circus World Museum, Baraboo, Wisconsin

and killed Old Bet, one of America's first circus elephants, after they decided that she was the reincarnation of the Behemoth mentioned in the Book of Job. The judge who ruled in favor of the defendants in another case, two New England teenagers who had around 1800 shot and killed another circus elephant for fun as she traveled a country road with her keepers on the way to her next performing engagement, summed up the public sentiment in his statement: "A elerphant is a dangersome varmint that hain't got no bizness arunning eround the country a-skeerin' of hosses an' a-frightenin wimmin an' children."

A century later, citizens of Erwin, Tennessee, tried and hanged the elephant Mary, who was visiting town with the Sparks-World Famous Shows, after she killed her keeper. Rumors about the outlandish and apparently deadly beast began to fly, and soon the local populace was certain that Mary had killed at least three, and perhaps as many as eighteen, people in a bloody rampage that had to be stopped. There was some suggestion that Mary, like Jumbo, might have been suffering from a painful tooth and also that the unfortunate keeper, Walter Eldridge, had mistreated her. Nevertheless, the Sparks Brothers Company agreed to destroy Mary—possibly against their better economic judgment, for the elephant was valued at $20,000 and should have performed well for another thirty years. Why Sparks Brothers chose to kill Mary as they did, rather than simply shoot her, remains unclear. Perhaps the potential for spectacle was too strong for showmen to resist, or perhaps the company felt the hysteria surrounding Eldridge's death was so strong that only a dramatic gesture would quell it. Mary was hanged from a railroad derrick on September 13, 1916. When the chain used to hoist Mary into the air snapped, the impact from the resulting fall stunned the elephant into a stuporous silence, and she offered little resistance when she was hanged a second time, successfully, before the expectant crowd.

In their modern incarnations, zoos and circuses differ little in their treatment and exhibition of elephants. Many elephants, particularly males, are called upon to travel as zoos investigate the problems of captive breeding and struggle to keep the gene pool viable among breeding animals. Also, zoos often train their (mostly Asian) elephants to perform crowd-pleasing tricks, and quite a few offer elephant rides. Although many conservationists and animal rights activists deplore such demeaning uses of the elephant, activities that occupy their minds and bodies, even in such unnatural ways, probably help captive elephants live healthier and somewhat happier lives. Such activities are certainly preferable to the miserable situation some zoo elephants still find themselves in: isolated from others of their kind in a small space only a few paces wide. Fortunately, zoo management has become much more enlightened, and as naturalistic spaces such as recreations of the African

Unlucky Mary, falsely accused of killing some eighteen people, was hung in Erwin, Tennessee, the town where she had been performing, in 1916. In reality, she killed only her keeper, who had mistreated her.

savannah become the norm, many captive elephants will lead more comfortable lives, though never with the full freedom to pursue the range of activities they enjoy in the wild.

THE MYSTICAL ELEPHANT

However many parts the elephant has played in human culture and history, the most enduring and consistent role has been as a spiritual force. The animal's physical invincibility may be responsible for a measure of the respect humans feel for the elephant, but their reverence probably has more to do with the elephant's character as observed through the ages. Interestingly, this creature that exhibits so many of the qualities we most admire when we detect them in ourselves—loyalty, altruism, playfulness, curiosity, affection—is almost always seen in a positive light wherever it appears in human mythologies and religions.

In the animist traditions of tribal Africans, animals (and many other aspects of nature) possess spiritual powers that can be transferred to, or captured by, human beings. This is why, when an animal has been hunted and killed, the hunters prize certain parts believed to be repositories for the animal's spiritual qualities and distribute them carefully among the members of their group. In the case of the elephant, considered a particularly powerful animal, special parts to be eaten may include the heart, trunk, and temporal gland. Generally, the hunter who felled the elephant might keep one tusk and present the other to the chief of his group as a tribute to his power. Other body parts, such as

© Alinari/Art Resource,NY

Hunted in North Africa and traded by the Romans from ports such as Ostia, where the mosaic on page 35 was discovered, the elephant retained an aura of mystery in the midst of commerce. Eventually, the animals came to be associated with eternal life, portrayed symbolically with candelabra or, as in this carving found in Rome, with torches, both symbolic of light and life.

the hair or tip of the trunk, are also collected and made into charms that will impart the qualities of the elephant—strength, endurance, fearlessness—to the wearer. Some tribes also search for a thorn or bit of wood that may be lodged in the temporal gland—an especially lucky find. Still other items, such as powdered ivory, considered a cure for acne, or fat from the heart, an aid to conception, are stored away as medicines until needed.

In the East, the elephant-headed god Ganesha is a central figure of Hinduism. Tales of how Ganesha got his elephant's head vary, but basically the story is this: Ganesha was guarding the door of his mother, the goddess Parvati, and turned away the demon-god Shiva, who desired to enter. Shiva was so angry that he cut off Ganesha's head with a single stroke and continued on to Parvati's chamber. The goddess in turn was so irate at what Shiva had done to her son that he was forced to make amends, but did so rather ungraciously (as gods often do when they are coerced). Depending on the source of the tale, Shiva either swore that Parvati's headless son could have the head of the first animal that passed by, or he sent his demons out to bring back the first head they could find. In the end, Ganesha acquired the head of an elephant, gaining, in his new life, a reputation for being intelligent, wise, and good-humored as well. Ganesha is the god from whom Hindus seek good fortune before the start of any intellectual endeavor, and his figure at the entrance to temples and shrines is reckoned to facilitate enlightenment. (In the Shinto tradition of Japan, the image of the elephant has similarly peaceful connotations.)

In the Buddhist tradition, which grew out of Hinduism, another story describes the birth of the Buddha as a historical person, Siddhārtha

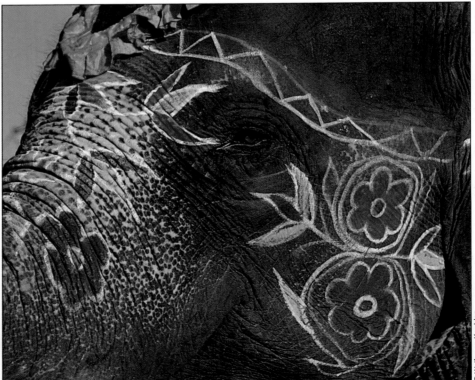

Painted and bejeweled elephants have long been part of Hindu and Buddhist religious processions, and "white elephants" with splotches of light pigmentation are especially revered in Thailand, where all such animals automatically belong to the king. Because of the elephant's endangered status, these traditions may one day soon live only in memory.

Gautama. As this tradition goes, in the sixth century A.D., a white elephant appeared to Queen Maya, Siddhārtha's mother, in a dream that was considered to be the moment of his conception. Should the Enlightened One physically return to earth again, Buddhist tradition asserts, it will be as an elephant.

These Hindu and Buddhist beliefs are at the heart of the reverence for white elephants in many Asian countries. In Thailand, for example, all white elephants—which, by the way, are not actually white, but have patches of lighter-than-usual pigmentation—are considered the property of the king. Whenever a white elephant is found in the wild, it is conveyed with great ceremony to the king's elaborate stables, where it will be bathed, perfumed, painted, bejeweled, and treated with respect for the rest of its life. The more such animals the king accumulates, the more prestige he earns, for his supply of wisdom is considered directly proportional to the number of white elephants he has. Priests close to the king watch his elephants very carefully for signs of any divine messages of which he should be apprised. Elsewhere, in Sri Lanka and Myanmar and India, for example, richly decorated elephants were once essential to most religious processions, but now, with the numbers of Asian elephants so precariously low, they are able to play this role only infrequently.

The Romans certainly never installed the elephant in their pantheon of gods, but even in their society the elephant's significance and roles surpassed that of war servant and plaything. The Romans believed that elephants worshipped Sol, the sun god, and often used the animals in processions as torch-bearers—literally the bearers of light and life. Roman artists, too, often depicted elephants with or near candelabra and this, in combination with their reputation for long life, eventually led to the use of the elephant's image on tombs as a symbol of life beyond the grave. Perhaps something of this Roman association of the elephant with the afterlife survives in a manuscript of Christian writings (*Bestiary,* Harleian manuscript 3244) compiled by a Greek monk of Alexandria and held by the British Museum, which reads, in part:

> *Then came the great elephant . . . the wise elephant, that is our Lord Jesus Christ. Greater than all, he is made the smallest of all. Being wounded he bore our infirmities and carried our sins.*

Even in the second youngest of the world's major religions the elephant earned a brief moment of reverence, again as a symbol of wisdom and peace, although today its association with Christ, the giver of eternal life, is largely forgotten.

The merry, wise Hindu god Ganesha turned his fortune from bad to good when he received his elephant head from the demon god Shiva. In Buddhist tradition, the elephant is associated with wisdom in the form of enlightenment.

© Gerry Ellis/The Wildlife Collection

chapter three

MOTHER KNOWS BEST

Better to live alone; with a fool there is no companionship. With few desires, live alone and do no evil, like an elephant in the forest, roaming at will.

—Suttapitaka, Dhammapada 23:330

n spite of civilization's long and close association with the elephant, many myths and outright slanders have persisted regarding its nature and behavior. For a long time elephant herds were said to be guided by a fierce old bull, reflecting society's own gender expectations rather than any true acquaintance with elephant habits. Destructive "rogue" elephants were greatly feared, and their senseless rampages against human beings and their property were thought to be the rule in elephant behavior rather than the exception. Some men held that the vegetarian elephant actually liked to dine on fish and mussels and—the most horrid thought— human flesh. Others insisted, romantically, that elephants mated for life and, perhaps feeling shy or a bit coy, only experienced sexual contact under cover of night. Perhaps the most stubbornly persistent myth of all was the elephant graveyard, a bone-littered sanctuary toward which all elephants supposedly gravitated when they felt their appointed hour drawing near, and from which humans could pick up gleaming ivory tusks more easily than they ever dreamed possible.

Still, from time to time, stories of a different tone drifted in from the plains and forest, usually from ivory hunters. The hunter, although the elephant's most feared enemy, was at the same time its closest intimate, simply because he had to spend time in the elephant's world in order to bring it down. In many of these stories respect and wonder are greatly in evidence, as in this description from *Kill: Or Be Killed* (1933), by Major W. Robert Foran, of an encounter with elephants in colonial Uganda:

> *I followed up that bull and his four loyal*
> *nurses for three most strenuous days, but never*
> *got a remote chance to finish him. Meanwhile,*
> *the rest of the herd had gone on their way in a*

Opposite page: Mother and the family are all to this young elephant calf. One of the many myths about elephant behavior recently disproved by ethologists studying elephants in the wild is the belief that bull elephants led the herd. In fact, adult bulls are solitary animals, and the herd is deeply matriarchal.

© Fritz Polking/M.L. Dembinsky Jr. Photography Assoc

Above: Elephants use their trunks and sense of smell to identify and greet each other. Comfort and affection seem to be essential ingredients in their communication with other members of the species.

Opposite page: Early European ivory hunters were impressed by elephants' detailed knowledge of the terrain within their home range.

different direction. The four cows never left their sorely wounded mate for a single moment. It was really astounding how fast and how far they travelled with him, for I knew that bull was mortally hurt.

Towards dusk on the third day I came up with them again. I was just in time to see the old tusker go down and die. For quite an hour the cows stood over his body, every now and then uniting in an effort to lift him on his feet. Finally they must have sensed that he was dead. They departed slowly, halting every few yards to look back at his prostrate body.

Frank Hulme Melland, in his 1938 account *Elephants in Africa,* was deeply impressed by the amount of time he had wasted trying to outwit a herd of elephants in the Luangwa Valley of Zambia:

We tried for years to find a better route [from the top of Muchinga escarpment—a 3,500-foot [1,050-m] sheer drop—to the valley], but we had to give it up and come back to the elephant path. It was not only the best way, it was the only practical way between the two levels. . . . On this escarpment they needed a regular route [to obtain musuku, "a fruit of which they are inordinately fond, which grows there in profusion and ripens at the Christmas season"] and found it, as a regular road engineer would.

The solitary ivory hunter Arthur Neumann recalled a profound impression of a different sort in his account of his career, *Elephant Hunting in East Equatorial Africa* (1898): "The bull fondled his mate with his trunk, and then, standing side by side, they crossed trunks and put the tips in each other's mouths, an undoubted elephantine kiss."

Melland, in his book, goes on to reveal many other naturalistic facts about the elephants of his acquaintance. Elephants, he writes, have a decided preference for certain cultivated crops (tall millet or sorghum, maize, beans, and bananas). They obtain salt by digging up anthills, and the dimensions of the cavities they leave in the course of this activity often reveal to hunters the size of an individual's tusks. Melland also writes that "although for very many years I have hunted both in Asia and Africa, I have never seen a sick elephant in the wild state"; and that

Stephen J. Kraseman/Valan Photos

Long feared as ferocious, irritable beasts, elephants at ease are actually fun-loving, easy-going creatures. Unless provoked, their chief danger to man is simply their huge size.

hurt elephants routinely plaster their wounds with mud or dust. And, he declares, it was "the 19th century lust for ivory that spoiled the elephant's nature," suggesting (as researchers in the field now confirm) that most instances of roguishness or ill-temper were caused by festering spear or bullet wounds, cruel treatment by trainers, or unnatural confinement, particularly during musth—all traceable to man rather than some unpredictable hostility in the elephant's character. A few ivory hunters of the early twentieth century were so affected by what they observed of the elephant's good nature that they gave up their profession, although publicly they usually chose to cloak such a decision in other explanations.

Determining which stories and rumors about elephants might be based on truth and which are plainly false has not been easy, even since the emergence in the twentieth century of ethology, the study of animal behavior, as a field of scientific endeavor. Elephants, being large, powerful, and willful, have never been ideal candidates for systematic study. Still, determination on the part of researchers has yielded much solid information, and the picture of elephant life that has emerged since 1965, when the Scottish zoologist Iain Douglas-Hamilton began observ-

ing elephants in the Lake Manyara area of Tanzania, confirms many of
the hunters' observations and refutes the myths. Elephants are indeed
gentle, highly intelligent, and bound for life to their families by strong
ties of affection. Their societies, geared toward passing on a great deal
of acquired knowledge, are as structured and orderly as the individuals
within them are unique.

By the late 1970s, when scientists had pieced together the basic life
cycle of the elephant, giant strides had been made in understanding an
animal often maligned or romanticized in the popular lore. Ethologists
arrived at this more complete understanding of the elephant by following the lives of individuals over time and recording the details of their
interactions with other individuals. The conditions of this research,
conducted in heat and isolation in the African bush, are not easy. To
start with, the scientists must learn to recognize each elephant in a
study population on sight. This is accomplished by photographing each
animal and noting certain identifying characteristics, such as holes,
tears, or the pattern of veins in the ear, or the size and shape of, and
any breaks in, the tusks. Only by making certain of the identity of each
individual in a study population and accumulating knowledge about
their lives based on detailed observation, can researchers possibly make
assumptions about the behaviors they observe and draw conclusions
from them.

As time goes on—and a continuous observation period over a group's
complete life cycle is essential for a holistic understanding of an animal
that lives as long as a human being—new subtleties and whole new areas
for research continue to emerge from the studies of Douglas-Hamilton,
Cynthia Moss, and Joyce Poole (Kenya), Rowan Martin (Zimbabwe), An-
thony Hall-Martin (South Africa), Katherine Payne (Cornell University),
and others in the field. Indeed, their discoveries about elephant social
organization, temperament, mating behavior, and communication shatter many long-held notions about the differences between humans and

*Ask now the beasts, and they shall teach
thee; and the fowls of the air, and they
shall tell thee.*

—Job 12:7

other animals. But time, however essential, may also be this work's greatest enemy, as researchers struggle to maintain continuity and integrity in their observations in the midst of shrinking habitats and among populations decimated and deeply disturbed by the ravages of poaching. As poaching escalated throughout the 1970s, it became evident that opportunities to observe stable elephant populations relatively unaffected by civilization were going to become increasingly rare. The more scientists learned, the more heart-rendingly obvious it became that, for those elephants that survived into the twenty-first century, the looming specter of a limited life spent in zoos or tightly controlled reserves would inevitably impoverish not only the wise, playful, freedom-loving elephant, but also our own experience of them.

An African elephant cow and her calf set off in search of the rest of their family, a group that usually consists of up to fifteen individuals.

ELEPHANT FAMILIES

In elephant society, no animal is more important than the matriarch. She is the hub, the brain center for her immediate associates—usually some six to fifteen female relatives and their calves who follow her in their daily travels, and look to her wisdom to sort out any troubles that arise. These troubles may be simple, such as when to eat or rest in the shade. Or they may be far more complex, including such concerns as: where to find a certain delicious fruit that only ripens on a few days each year; how to stay as far away as possible from poachers; where to find water when all the temporary sources and most of the usual permanent ones have dried up in a year of severe drought; how to handle unruly adolescent males who disrupt the daily life of the herd and present the undesirable prospect of inbreeding. Researchers confirm that the solutions to many of these problems are learned rather than instinctual, making the matriarch, above all, the ultimate repository of essential survival knowhow that younger animals simply would not have had time to learn on their own. Like humans, elephants need a long childhood and adolescence in which to learn these critical skills from their elders.

The matriarch attains her position in the usual way of the animal kingdom, that is, by establishing dominance over the other members of her group. This occurs chiefly through repeated displays of aggression, in which the eventual matriarch asserts her claim by successfully imposing her will on her companions and refusing to be pushed around by them. There may be some hereditary component, with daughters inheriting their temperament and thus their position from their mothers, but this is not always true. Sometimes when a matriarch dies, an elephant family may split up permanently, or temporarily until the question of leadership has been decided.

Besides holding her own family together, the matriarch is the decision maker in terms of which other elephants the members of her band will associate with most closely. Scientists have observed that matriarchs seem to have close ties to certain other family groups; these families may travel, eat, sleep, and play together for a few days at a time or for longer periods. Such bond or kinship groups are well acquainted and seem to enjoy each other's company. The groups go through an elaborate process (as do individual elephants) of greeting each other with rumbles and squeaks when they are first reunited. A strong-smelling fluid streams from the temporal glands located just behind each animal's eye; the animals also may run about in tight circles while urinating and defecating—sure signs of excitement among elephants.

Researchers have noticed that the ties between such kinship groups often become much weaker, or even fall away completely, when a matriarch dies. Unfortunately, scientists can still only speculate about the nature and origins of such ties, since they have not yet observed elephants long enough to trace the development of these bonds. Most scientists believe that the bond groups must be related through the

An elephant family is headed by a matriarch, an older cow who has proven her mastery of the local terrain by surviving to a mature age and assumes the mantle of leadership by imposing her will on the female members of her group when the former matriarch begins to fail or dies.

matriarch, perhaps dating back over several generations. This is only one of the many questions scientists may not be able to answer until they have been able to observe the elephants of a single generation through most of their sixty- or seventy-year life spans.

In addition to functioning as a repository of communal knowledge, elephant families are highly efficient nurseries. When a female elephant is ready to give birth, she may choose to go off to an isolated place in the bush to complete her labor alone. Sometimes, though, she is accompanied by another female or two who may assist her, in a kind of midwifery, by removing the fetal membranes from the newborn and encouraging her in the straining and walking that expels the afterbirth.

The new elephant baby can normally stand within twenty minutes or so after birth, although help is usually necessary from its mother. A first

© Walt Anderson/Visuals Unlimited

The matriarch leads her family on daily foraging trips and assumes the duty of deciding when to fight or flee danger.

attempt at suckling follows soon after, and within an hour the calf may be ready to accompany its mother back to her family group with some assistance. An elephant that has calved usually recovers her strength fairly quickly. If the mother is more than usually exhausted, another member of her family, perhaps one of the older calves who serve a very important role as "nannies" or "aunts" to the young ones, may stay close by to fondle and reassure the infant.

A young elephant is rarely out of reach of the mother's strong, guiding trunk in the early months of its life. She encourages the baby, helps it keep up with the other members of the herd, and often pulls it back if it starts to stray. The baby is dependent upon its mother's milk for the first two years of life, but soon after birth the calf becomes curious

Left: Baby elephants soon learn to love water, a necessity for keeping cool in the hot savannahs. The youngsters' play, especially sparring to test physical strength, helps them to learn their place in elephant society.

about the many plants it will soon begin to nibble on toward the end of his first year. In a characteristic gesture, the calf may put the tip of its trunk into the mother's mouth, in order to better analyze the plants she eats. (Later on, the elephant will use the same gesture to greet and recognize the members of other herds, employing its sense of smell.) Also, if the water supply is out of the calf's range, the mother siphons water in her trunk and pours it down her baby's throat.

All adult elephants are very solicitous of the youngsters' safety, and at the first sign of a threatening force such as a lion, the adults draw close together in a laager formation with the young ones in the center for protection. Older and adolescent calves in the family show a strong interest in the newborns from the start. As the babies grow stronger and are allowed a bit more freedom to explore, these aunts, actually older siblings or cousins, take over many caretaking duties from new mothers. This not only gives the mother a welcome break from the constant attendance young calves require, but allows the aunts to gradually learn the skills they will need in a few years when they too become mothers.

Early on, a favorite activity of calves is sparring and playing. Young male calves, particularly, enjoy pushing and shoving each other to test their strength, a behavior they will use later to establish their place in the dominance ranking that occurs among all the male elephants in the area. The youngsters also enjoy kicking up a ruckus in a mud puddle, games of tag, and many other forms of play in which elephants continue to indulge during much of their long lives. One of the most thrilling sights in nature must be a group of elephants, young and old alike, rolling in the dust, cavorting under the trees or in the water, and "being silly," as Cynthia Moss terms their play in her book *Elephant Memories: Thirteen Years in the Life of an Elephant Family.*

Below: Not only the mother but the entire herd is responsible for the care of young elephants. From their elders, the youngsters acquire the knowledge of obtaining food and water supplies that will help ensure the group's survival in future lean years.

Puberty, which occurs at about age fourteen, means an abrupt change for young elephant bulls. Probably to prevent inbreeding and the disturbances of constant sparring, the matriarch gradually pushes young bulls out of the family group. Thereafter, much of the bulls' lives are spent in solitude—a sharp contrast to the communal life they enjoyed previously.

As it is for human beings, puberty is a time of great change for elephants. When young males reach the age of thirteen or fourteen, their mock sparring starts to become intrusive in the life of the elephant herd. Perhaps sensing that such roughhousing could interfere with the care and protection of youngsters, the matriarch begins to chase these adolescent males away. At first, the growing males don't know how to interpret this, so they keep returning to the herd. But the matriarch always drives them away again, and their returns gradually become of shorter duration. Finally, at about age sixteen, male elephants separate from their families, and strike out on the essentially solitary existence they will lead for the rest of their lives.

Some observers report that an older bull may sometimes seem to take a younger one under his wing, and may pass on some of his knowledge of local conditions now that the young bull no longer has a matriarch to look to. More frequently, two or more high-spirited young males take up with each other for a few days, alternately feeding and sparring to test their rank. This is an important activity, because each sexually mature male must establish his dominance relative to the other males in the area in order to claim his right to mate with receptive females. The higher a bull's rank, the more frequent his opportunities to pass on his

When elephants fight it is the grass that suffers.

—Kikuyu proverb (Kenya)

genes; all lesser bulls will defer to him when a female is in estrus (the time when an egg is released and ready for fertilization). Very occasionally, researchers say, when conditions are particularly good, a large number of bulls may come together for a period of feeding and socializing. But all these alliances are temporary, and though bulls may return from time to time to visit their original family groups for a day or two, they are never again part of a permanent group.

Much of a grown male elephant's time and energy is spent looking for females to mate with. When a female elephant comes into estrus for the first time at about age twelve, young bulls travel from miles around to be near her and try to mate with her. The males are assisted in the quest by their acute sense of smell, and they constantly test the urine of the females with their trunks for the presence of a pheromone produced throughout the estrous cycle. Because she has never experienced estrus before, the wave of attention can be quite disconcerting to a young female. The bulls will chase her mercilessly and quite a few of them may mate with her, until she appears very harried. The members of her family join in the excitement by trumpeting loudly each time one of the males is successful and making a general commotion.

If the young cow is lucky, an older, clearly dominant male, a musth bull, will find her and chase away her pesky suitors. The heightened levels of testosterone in a musth bull make him unusually aggressive and give him priority over all the other nonmusth bulls, regardless of his normal ranking within the local hierarchy. Bulls do not usually come into musth until their late thirties and they must be in peak physical condition to do so. The older a bull, the longer his period of musth may last—sometimes up to three months each year—giving him a lengthy period in which he does not have to compete for mates except with a few other bulls whose musth period overlap with his own.

Ethologists theorize that females prefer musth bulls because they are older, larger animals and therefore more likely to produce long-lived progeny with the intelligence to survive difficult periods in the bush. But there is also a more immediate and practical reason why females prefer a musth bull: After their mating(s), he stays with her, and guards or escorts her until the end of her estrous cycle, which provides her with some days of calm, free from male attentions, in which, hopefully, she will conceive. This is the ideal situation, but it may not occur on the first try. A breeding female may have to experience several estrous cycles before she learns to resist the insistent male attention until a musth bull appears.

A fertile elephant cow will give birth fairly regularly throughout her life, usually at intervals of four or five years. Estrus, however, may vary widely in its frequency, and the females' cycles are closely attuned to

This young bull could have damaged his right tusk while testing his dominance ranking in a sparring match with another bull. Since truly violent fights between elephants are rare, it is more likely that he broke it in the course of normal wear: Elephants, like left- or right-handed humans, tend to favor one tusk over another.

© Fritz Polking/M.L. Dembinsky Jr. Photography Assoc.

Opposite page: At about age thirty-five an elephant bull begins coming into musth, a condition of heightened hormonal activity that lasts for several months each year. Musth makes the bull unusually aggressive and ready to fight off all competitors, and gives him an edge over the nonmusth bulls in winning the right to mate.

environmental conditions. In particularly harsh, dry years, cows whose youngest calves are at least two or three years old may not come into estrus at all, and resume their cycles only after conditions and food supply improve.

An aging cow's birth rate slows down after the age of fifty or fifty-five, and with good reason. Around this time an elephant's last set of molars usually erupts; as these teeth gradually wear down and as feeding becomes more and more difficult, the animal, whether cow or bull, inevitably nears the end of its life. As humans often do, an aged animal may seem less interested in the life of the group, and an older matriarch will gradually withdraw to the periphery of her family's life, allowing the more dominant cows to begin to vie for her role.

An elephant's natural death is probably one of the least harsh in the animal kingdom, where eat or be eaten is the prevailing rule. If an animal has survived hunters and poachers, and avoided becoming mired in the occasional merciless mudslick, in extreme old age its physical condition will just gradually decline. Eventually the elephant weakens to the point where it can no longer travel with the other members of its herd and may seek a convenient refuge near water. Finally, alone and perhaps only half conscious, it will lose the battle against starvation and return to the earth. Other elephants, if they witness the animal's death or find its body afterward, will gather around it, swaying and touching their former companion with their trunks. The elephants may try to lift the animal with their tusks and may keep up their vigil for several days. Eventually, as Major Foran observed, they seem to recognize that the animal they know so well is gone for good, and they may pile dirt or leaves or brush upon the body before drifting away with many backward glances.

Months or years later, elephants coming upon the remains of a former compatriot will linger with the bones in seeming remembrance, nudging them with their trunks as if trying to identify the individual, and perhaps scattering them about the area. Although scientists have uncovered no evidence of any sort of elephant graveyard, the survivors frequently —and for no logical, scientific reason anyone has been able to discern— pick up the dead elephant's tusks in their trunks and shatter the ivory against a rock or a nearby tree.

One of the most stringent admonitions among ethologists is the importance of not anthropomorphizing about the animals whose behaviors they study. But many people who have observed these last rites, particularly those in the field who have also witnessed the great care and joy with which elephants conduct their lives together, will tell you that elephants grieve for their own just as surely as men, women, and children do.

Bringing Up Baby

Raising a baby elephant requires all the commitment and close contact involved in raising a human child.

Daphne Sheldrick first became a parent at the age of three. The young *dikdik* (a tiny antelope) she adopted as a girl was the first of many orphaned animals she has raised during a lifetime spent in Kenya, much of it as the wife of game warden David Sheldrick. By her own reckoning, Daphne Sheldrick has "raised most species" found in East Africa; in the process she has gained a reputation for succeeding with the most delicate and demanding cases—particularly young elephants and rhinos orphaned by poachers—where others might have given up.

Since her husband's sudden death in 1977, Sheldrick has continued practicing her unusual art from her home at the edge of Nairobi National Park. Her charges frequently include infant elephants, which she and a team of devoted keepers nurture with the same intensity the animals' original families would have. "The secret of raising baby elephants," Sheldrick explains, "is that first of all, the people who look after them have to replace the families they have lost. They must be with them twenty-four hours a day, because little elephants are never on their own in a wild situation—the whole herd cares for them. Having lost a family once, they come in very traumatized and go through a very bad period of grieving that sometimes costs them their lives." When an elephant grieves, Sheldrick says, "it has nightmares, it screams and cries, it can't sleep—all these things—in the same way that a human grieves.

"Elephants are very human animals," she continues. "We think about them in human

A baby elephant is completely dependent on its mother's milk for the first year of its life and relies on it heavily during the second. One of the most important breakthroughs in raising orphaned elephants has been Daphne Sheldrick's development of a formula with a fat content that under-one-year-olds can digest.

terms. Their development is parallel to ours, and they are probably more sensitive. They are extremely compassionate, caring animals, also extremely intelligent. So we have to relate to these little babies, and they *are* just infants, in human terms, in order to understand what's going on. Some of them have seen their entire family mowed down at once and the ivory hacked from their faces. If you can't relate to them, it's not possible to interpret why they're doing something, what they need, and so on.''

In this nursery stage of their upbringing, keepers accompany the babies from dawn to dawn, leading them out of the stable for a first feeding at the start of each new day. As long as they are drinking milk, the youngsters must be fed every three hours without fail. For many years, elephants under two years old always defeated Sheldrick's tender loving care, since most commercial formulas contained cow's milk, whose fat the babies were unable to assimilate. Finally, after years of trial and error, she discovered a formula for sensitive human babies that was based on coconut oil, and soon she had a first survivor from among the very youngest orphans. Getting the young elephants to nurse properly is

To simulate mother's comforting presence, the keepers in Daphne Sheldrick's orphanage remain within trunk's reach of the babies at all times. Tarpaulins take the place of adult elephants' protective bulk when the youngsters need protection from cold and damp.

© Kenneth Garrett/FPG International

not only a matter of presenting a bottle of the proper formula. The ambience must be properly reassuring, so comforting physical contact—particularly involving the trunk—with a loved keeper is vital if a young orphan is to thrive.

Feeding certainly is most important, but the keepers must also replace Mother and the herd in every other way, which is a very physical routine. The keepers must take the baby elephants out into the woods to play, help them learn to eat leaves and grasses, assist them with mud baths, check their temperature, and bundle them up in blankets and tarpaulins if they become chilled or damp. The keepers rotate night duty, sleeping with the elephants in their hay-filled stalls in special bunks designed to keep the men within trunk's reach at all times.

At about the age of two, the young elephants are weaned and transferred to a mixed-species orphan herd in Tsavo East National Park. The leader of this unusual herd, which has included zebras and rhinos as well as elephants, is Eleanor, an orphaned elephant whom Sheldrick helped to raise almost thirty years ago. The babies make the transition, again, with the help of a loved keeper, who accompanies them to their new home and family closer to the wild. In about fifteen years, the young males will leave Eleanor's herd to take up the solitary life of bulls, just as they would if they had remained with their own families. The females remain behind with Eleanor in their own matriarchal unit.

Eleanor is not particularly special, Sheldrick claims, for having signed on for unusual maternal duties, since ''all female elephants are like that.'' She *is* different, however, than the other orphans that came before her in that she has voluntarily chosen to maintain her links with human beings. ''The reason for that is quite easy to understand,'' Sheldrick says. ''Unlike the other elephants, she didn't join the wild herds at puberty because another little elephant came in who was about a year old. That was the youngest elephant I'd managed to raise before we got the formula right,

© Starr Osolinski/M.L. Dembinsky Jr. Photography Assoc.

and I didn't feed him milk, but managed to raise him on cereals. Eleanor stayed to look after this calf because he was so dependent on us, and became a leader in her own right. Status is very important to all elephants, not just the bulls. Eleanor is a leader, she considers herself to be a leader, but she can't be a leader in a wild situation—she's far too young. So Eleanor prefers to stay with the orphan herd, but she does go with the wild elephants often and takes the orphans with her and brings them back. She has more stature that way."

If Eleanor is simply an ordinary elephant, the keepers Sheldrick works with are just ordinary human beings. "Since most wildlife here is now compressed within national parks, most of these men have never even seen an elephant," she says. "You just have to train them to communicate with the animal, to understand what it's doing, and to relate to it in a human way." Not all such relationships work out, however. "You just stand back and watch," Sheldrick explains. "If the elephant doesn't like his keeper after a month you know he never will. And you take that man out and start again."

What is the friendship between humans and a baby elephant like? "Same as between two people basically," Sheldrick says, then adds after a moment, "It's for life."

Eventually, the young orphans will be returned to the wild. After the high poaching rates of the 1980s, Sheldrick considers the survival of every individual elephant to be of the utmost importance to the survival of the species.

chapter four

THE SECRETS OF ELEPHANT COMMUNICATION

The most beautiful thing we can experience is the mysterious. It is the only source of true art and science, and he to whom this emotion is a stranger, he who can no longer pause and wonder or stand rapt in awe—he is already half dead. His eyes are shut.

**—Albert Einstein,
Ideas and Opinions**

F or those acquainted with elephants—hunters, game wardens, and later, scientists—the way individuals and groups of elephants separated by several miles often seemed to decide to take a certain simultaneous action presented a perplexing mystery. How did elephant families know that seasonal rains had begun to refresh a distant part of their range and begin migrating concurrently in that direction? And how did bulls, who almost never come into contact with females in their daily routines, manage to find a receptive mate on the three or four days in a five-year period when she was fertile? What caused a herd, grazing peacefully, to stop suddenly and stand motionless for long moments with their heads held high and their ears wide? The hunters and game wardens tended to dismiss these coincidences as evidence of some mysterious power in elephants—perhaps the elephant equivalent of ESP. Scientists continued to sift through what they had been able to find out about elephant behavior in hopes of uncovering an answer, but the answer remained elusive.

These questions might have remained a mystery had it not been for a 1984 visit Katharine B. Payne, a researcher at Cornell University in Ithaca, New York, whose specialty was the low-frequency songs of whales, made to the elephant house in Portland, Oregon's Washington Park Zoo. Absorbed in watching three female Asian elephants with their newborn calves, Payne nevertheless noticed something peculiar about the atmosphere. As she watched, the air around her seemed to throb

Opposite page: Elephants have amazed many observers with their seemingly uncanny knowledge of faraway events. Now, researchers are beginning to uncover some important aspects of their extraordinary ability to communicate over long distances, among them infrasonic vocalizations and chemical messages in the form of pheromones.

rhythmically, as though a loud noise were being produced. However, the animals apparently were producing no forceful sound, just the usual contented mother-calf rumbles.

The memory of this peculiar sensation continued to nag at Payne once she returned to Cornell, and a few months later she returned to the zoo with two colleagues to test a hypothesis. It had occurred to her that the elephants, like the whales she knew so well, might have been producing low-frequency, or infrasonic, calls—many of which consisted of sounds below the range of human hearing. The tape the team made of clearly audible elephant calls yielded paydirt: when replayed at a faster speed, more than three times as many elephant calls became audible. Research revealed that a zoologist at San Diego Wild Animal Park, Judith Kay Berg, had published her findings about the same sorts of calls a couple of years earlier, but so far no one had followed up on what they might mean for elephant communication.

Payne was intrigued, and so were other researchers in the field in Africa, who immediately saw in her findings the implications for the mysterious behaviors that had puzzled them so. Infrasound, as we know from such natural phenomena as earthquakes and thunder, travels over vast distances—as much as twelve miles (19 km), much farther than higher-pitched sounds. And, it turns out, infrasound is not dissipated by passage through the dense forests and woodlands that comprise some elephant habitats. Perhaps those mysterious convergences in elephant behavior that had been so puzzling were something much more straightforward than ESP after all.

Following her hypothesis, Payne and others began several research projects that involved elephants and infrasound. In Kenya's Amboseli National Park during 1985 and 1986, Payne and Joyce Poole recorded over a thousand elephant calls that confirmed that the African species also produced infrasonic calls. With colleague Bill Langbauer and others, Payne next went to Etosha, a large, open semidesert park in Namibia, to try and establish whether elephants did in fact respond to the low-frequency calls she had noticed. In a series of experiments carried out in 1986 and 1987, these scientists observed groups of elephants from a specially built observation tower and, from time to time, transmitted elephant calls recorded during Payne's visits to Amboseli. Careful notetaking on the timing of these calls, and videotapes of the elephants' behavior before and after the calls were broadcast, enabled the researchers to establish whether the calls seemed to elicit changes in behavior.

At the end of their time in Etosha, the team had observed that playbacks of infrasound calls known as contact calls (which families seem to use to keep in touch with each other) caused groups of female elephants to freeze, lift their heads, and spread their ears in a listening

Gerry Ellis/The Wildlife Collection

posture, before they responded with their own contact answer calls. Adult male elephants in Etosha, treated to a tape-recorded call made by a female in estrus, would head for the loudspeaker with the same purposeful stride repeatedly observed in male elephants setting out to find and court a receptive female. Moreover, the calls seemed to produce responses over distances of at least two and a half miles (4 km).

Payne's next project, begun in 1989, was a collaboration with Rowan Martin in Zimbabwe's Sengwa Wild Life Research Area. For many years Martin has recorded the movements and migratory paths of elephants using radio collars. His work established that elephant herds often take parallel, apparently coordinated paths in their daily wanderings even though they might be separated by as much as five miles (8 km); this suggested that the elephants must somehow be communicating with each other. By adding microphones and recording equipment to the Sengwa elephants' radio collars, Martin and Payne hope to establish that infrasound is the means by which the herds keep each other informed of their movements.

Joyce Poole and her colleagues Norah Njiraine and Soila Sayialel have continued to record calls and observe the behavior of the elephants at Amboseli. They have added a number of infrasound calls and infrasound components of higher-frequency calls to the vocabulary of about twenty-five elephant calls audible to humans that they had noted before Katharine Payne's discovery. Building on a formidable knowledge of the relationships, histories, and personalities of almost seven hundred elephants (a population also largely unaffected by the disturbances of poaching), the Amboseli Elephant Research Project is probably the most likely research project to give us a comprehensive knowledge of the way elephant language works in the wild.

Thunder, like many elephant vocalizations, contains many infrasound components. Scientists theorize that these components may tell an elephant herd when it is time to begin moving toward a distant part of their range where the rainy season has begun and fresh grasses are available.

MUSTH: COMMUNICATION BY SCENT AND SOUND

Besides opening the way for fascinating new studies of elephant language, the discovery of infrasound calls sheds considerable light on what was already known about elephant mating behavior. Cynthia Moss and Joyce Poole had been excited to discover in the late 1970s evidence of the phenomenon of musth in the African elephants they observed. Some of the older bulls in Amboseli, they noticed, at certain times seemed extremely aggressive and walked with purposeful strides in a peculiar stance with their heads held high. They also had copious secretions from the temporal glands located just behind each eye and constantly dribbled strong-smelling urine; over time the constant moisture caused the growth of a fungus that gave the elephants' penises a greenish color. (Analysis of the urine revealed that such bulls had higher levels of the male hormone testosterone than usual.) At first, the two scientists thought the bulls must be diseased, but they soon made the connection between these "symptoms" and observations made earlier about Asian bull elephants in musth.

Although musth in Asian elephants was associated with the reproductive cycle, scientists had long felt that its role was disruptive, a maladaptation that caused bulls to behave so aggressively that the cows, frightened, resisted their overtures. Poole, however, observed that among African elephants, the experienced cows seemed to prefer musth bulls, and put off the younger, more inept animals attracted to them during estrus. Because studies of African elephants in the wild far outnumber comparable studies of Asian elephants, scientists are still not certain why female Asian and African elephants should react so differently to musth bulls. Perhaps, being rather distantly related, the two species are simply different. Another logical explanation, however, is that most Asian bulls in musth have been observed under conditions far different from the freedoms they enjoy in the wild. It may be that their extreme aggression is less a function of their being in musth than the fact that they are simultaneously in musth *and* confined in jungle work camps, or in circuses and zoos (perhaps with no female companions at all), unable to fulfill their normal impulse to range far and seek out receptive mates. Until similar studies are conducted among Asian elephants, there is no way to interpret this behavior with certainty.

Scientists do know that both Asian and African elephant bulls that come into contact with cows constantly test the females' urine and genitals with their sensitive trunks for the presence of a pheromone that indicates whether the females are in estrus. Additionally, the discovery of musth and the way it functions has helped to clarify many puzzles regarding elephant sexual behavior. For instance, the pungent urine trails of musth bulls helped these aggressive animals avoid each other in the same way they located estrus females—through their sense of smell. Rather than fighting it out each time an estrous female was available, the males developed an elaborate hierarchy based on dominance that assured the strongest animals more frequent opportunities to pass on their genes. Musth played a crucial role in this system because it conferred upon those bulls who had proved their superiority by reaching an advanced age the most opportunities to mate. In fact, Moss and Poole felt there was some indication that the females of a population themselves came into estrus in response to certain males' habit of coming into musth during the same two- or three-month period each year.

None of these observations, however, really addressed the key question: How do male and female animals who spend most of their lives apart—usually many miles apart—find each other at the brief and crucial time when conception can take place? The discovery of ultrasound calls, it turned out, at last seemed to provide an answer. According to Katharine Payne, female elephants in estrus produce a special ultrasound song, in which "slow, deep rumbles, rising gently, become

Both infrasound and pheromones play a crucial role in bringing together a fertile elephant cow with a musth bull, who can guard her from unwanted male attentions until she conceives.

© Ken Cole

Elephant bulls in Namibia began walking with the purposeful stride reserved for finding mates toward a loudspeaker that broadcast the estrus songs of elephant cows that Katharine Payne had recorded in Kenya.

© Fritz Polking/M.L. Dembinsky Jr. Photography Assoc.

stronger and higher in pitch, then sink down again to silence at the end." Each such song may go on for a half hour, Payne says, and without fail, the female is soon surrounded by eager males. If none of these suitors is a musth male, the loud performance of the receptive cow's female relatives, who vocalize enthusiastically when the young bulls try to mate with her, also contains ultrasound components that may travel the necessary distance to attract a suitable musth bull to her side. Although the female chorus had been noted before, the discovery of infrasound calls provided the key to its significance.

Intraspecies Communication

In a way, these exciting discoveries about the ways elephants communicate with each other, like scientists' conclusions about other elephant behaviors, have the slightly eerie quality of a long-felt truth confirmed. After all, humans have recorded what they "know" about elephants

since before Aristotle's time. Now that scientists have devoted themselves to the study of elephants, many of these early observations turn
out to have been surprisingly accurate.

One area that undoubtedly will receive a great deal more study is the
area of elephant intelligence and, perhaps, creativity. Certainly there is
no shortage of reports—from earliest times, and from mahouts, zoo
keepers, philosophers, and historians—about the elephant's intelligence
and facility in communicating with humans. Asian elephants have reportedly outwitted their trainers in an endless assortment of ways, from
stuffing mud in the bells they wore to rewrapping their ankles in chains
from which they had broken free, apparently to keep their mahouts
from discovering their nighttime ramblings in search of their favorite
foods that humans eat.

When appropriate, elephants also may use their wit to correct a keeper's shortcomings. H. H. Scullard, in *The Elephant in the Greek and
Roman World* (1974), relates that:

. . . on the authority of a philosopher, Hagnon of Tarsus, Plutarch [Moralia, de Solleria Anima- lium, 12, 968] tells how an elephant in Syria, feeling that its keeper was stealing half its barley ration, carefully made two piles of it one day to make the thief aware that he knew. Another ras- cally keeper stole part of the ration and put stones under the remainder to make the pile look normal and deceive his master: the elephant took revenge by flinging with its trunk a mass of sand into the keeper's pot of porridge.

Such acts show a remarkable psychological understanding among ele- phants of both themselves and their keepers.

Several Western observers have found Asian work elephants so skilled at their jobs that they concluded that more than simply performing a task, such as bridge building or logging by rote, the animals must under- stand the principles underlying the work they had been trained to do— a conclusion perhaps rather obvious to the mahouts who trained them. And a rhinoceros researcher in Nepal who rode Asian elephants through the long grass, the better to observe his subjects in the course of his field work, reported with admiration how his mount stopped and refused to go further until he discovered that the notebook with all his data had fallen to the ground. Somehow, the animal had surmised some- thing of the notebook's importance.

None of this should be too surprising, since, as Sylvia K. Sikes puts it in *The Natural History of the African Elephant:*

The brain of the adult African elephant is the heaviest and largest of any living or extinct ter- restrial mammal. . . . A close examination of the elephant brain, however, combined with actual experience of living elephants in the wild and in captivity, yields abundant evidence that the ele- phant both possesses the mechanism and demon- strates the capacity for intelligence.

Obviously, such intelligence comes into play in work elephants' ability to comprehend human language; these animals commonly learn at least sixty words, and they respond to them appropriately when they are spoken in new combinations, an indication that such elephants under- stand at least the rudiments of syntax.

Reports that elephants have tried to turn their knowledge of human language into a two-way communication go back at least to Roman times. Edward Topsell, for instance, included in his 1607 volume *The Historie of Foure-Footed Beasts* the following account:

> Mutiannus *who was thrice Consul affirmed to* Pliny *that he saw an Elephant which learned the Greek letters, and was able with his tongue [trunk?] to write these words: Autos egoo Tadegrapsa laphura tekelt anetheca: that is, I wrote these things and dedicated the Celtic spoils: but in these actions of writing, the hand of the teacher must be also present to teach him how to frame the letters....*

More recently—and in a more personal communication—in 1983 TASS, the Soviet news agency, reported that a zoo elephant in the republic of Kazakhstan was said to have vocalized the following in an apparent demonstration of human speech: 'Batir is good', 'Batir is a fine fellow', 'Water', 'Have you given water to the elephant?' Certainly such statements are no more amazing than the reply the gorilla Koko, trained in Ameslan (sign language) by researcher Francine Patterson, gave a reporter who inquired whether she were a man or an animal: ''Fine animal gorilla.'' The difference, presumably—since no scientist seems to have followed up on Batir's reported accomplishment—is that the ele-

Elephants have always had a complex relationship with human beings. Now the question remains: Can we communicate with each other?

© John Shaw/Tom Stack & Associates

Among the many tricks taught to zoo elephants, painting for visitors has recently become popular. Yet the intriguing possibility exists that elephants create images on their own, without human intervention—possibly for reasons similar to human artists. Further investigation of this inclination in elephants could shed light on our understanding of the very nature of art.

phant picked up both a human language and the ability to vocalize it on his own.

Still other reported elephant behaviors hint at a realm of sensitivity that is beyond mere intelligence and approaches emotional complexity, a capacity we tend to think of as exclusively human. Examples of such behavior are the many reports of tears in captive elephants that have lost a companion, been mistreated, or punished after failing to master a circus routine. Another example is the elephant's apparent appreciation of music as reported by, among others, the Persian Abu al-Fazl ibn Mubarak in his *Ain i Akbori* (translated 1873): "[The elephant] learns to remember such melodies as can only be remembered by people acquainted with music." The Roman rhetorician Aelian also saw in the dancing of show elephants a genuine appreciation of the pipe playing to which they performed. One Roman-kept elephant who endured severe scoldings when she didn't learn a dance as well as her partners reportedly used to practice alone by moonlight, with no encouragement from her trainer.

Just what emotional and even artistic capacities elephants have is the subject of *To Whom It May Concern: An Investigation of the Art of Elephants,* an intriguing book written by David Gucwa and James Ehmann in 1985. While working as a keeper at the Burnet Park Zoo in Syracuse, New York, Gucwa noticed that his charge, an adolescent Asian elephant named Siri, frequently used a pebble to scratch patterns on the floor of her enclosure. Curious, Gucwa gathered pencils, paint, brushes, and drawing paper and presented them to Siri. Without instruction or reward, Siri investigated their properties and, pencil in trunk, soon began drawing images on a pad of paper held in Gucwa's lap. After accumulating several hundred of these images, which Siri often retraced with her trunk as if contemplating the merits of what she had created, Gucwa and his coauthor set about showing the drawings—frequently without revealing Siri's identity—to a number of artists, critics, ethologists, and other scientists who had expressed an interest in animal intelligence. Reactions ranged from the faintly raised eyebrows of other zookeepers, who agreed that their own elephants often doodled with a stick or pebble, but insisted that this was nothing but an idle reflex indicative of boredom, to enthusiastic responses from abstract expressionists Jerome Witkin and Willem de Kooning, whose comment on learning that Siri had produced the drawings was, "That's a damned talented elephant!"

One drawing in particular, which they called "To Whom It May Concern," captivated Gucwa and Ehmann and provided the title for their book. Other observers seemed attracted to this work also, and a Buddhist nun to whom they showed it immediately bowed to the image.

Given the elephant's respected position within the religions of the Far East, the nun's explanation that the drawing was the Chinese character for Buddha further confirmed Gucwa and Ehmann's sense that there was something special about Siri's work and about "To Whom It May Concern" in particular. Later, an Austrian-born Hindu monk and professor of anthropology at Syracuse University, Agehananda Bharati, made a suggestion, reported in *To Whom It May Concern,* that added yet another potential layer of meaning to Siri's powerful image. "You must forget," Bharati said:

> *the possibility of its being a pictograph and see if it's not some nongraphemic symbolism—that it's not a written sign but might represent some kind of* original *symbol which animals share with human beings.*
>
> *On that assumption—which I doubt very much, but without it we cannot proceed anywhere; the 90 percent possibility is that it's purely accidental, just a scribble, a movement of her trunk; 90 percent, and I want this down, because I don't want to get into trouble with my colleagues—but the other 10 percent ties in with the Jungian notion of an archetypal universe, which is of course shared between at least the higher animals and human beings.*

From Bharati's point of view, the proper question about Siri's or any other elephant's drawing is not necessarily whether it is art, but a more subtle, and perhaps more rewarding, inquiry into the origins of what humans tend to think of as their own private realm, that is, the world of consciousness.

Zoo politics and a long-overdue renovation of the Burnet Park Zoo, which sent Siri to live temporarily at the zoo in Buffalo, prevented David Gucwa from following up on his work with Siri. But the debate raised by the investigation he conducted with James Ehmann regarding the nature of Siri's drawings made one thing clearer than ever: Because of elephants' ability to communicate with unusual complexity, humans may be able to learn more from elephants about their (and our) nature than from any other animal. If our appreciation of elephants as fascinating creatures in and of themselves is not enough to focus our own energies and intelligence on saving them from extinction, perhaps our curiosity and the realization that we may be losing, forever, a valuable source of information will be.

© FPG International

chapter five

TRAGIC PAST, UNCERTAIN FUTURE

If the elephant vanished the loss to human laughter, wonder and tenderness would be a calamity.

V.S. Pritchett, in a review of The Roots of Heaven

magine, in the last hushed hour of the East African day, a group of elephants stepping silently through the brush and high grass on a well-worn path to the river. The only sounds as the gentle beasts head for the water and a last drink before nightfall are birdsong and the penetrating rasp of cicadas, elicited by the swiftly descending coolness. In a small clearing almost at the river's edge, the matriarch suddenly stops, spreads her ears wide in recognition of danger, and signals the others to move out as quickly as possible. The small band of nine turns in panic, beginning to run, but it is too late: A group of fellow creatures, also silent and better armed, has preceded them down the path.

Four poachers rush from the concealing brush and open fire with their G3 automatic rifles; in a few short minutes it is all over for the elephant family. The gunmen and their accomplices close in quickly, hacking with *panga*s, the multipurpose African machete, and a lone chainsaw the ivory from the seven prone elephants old enough to have tusks. Within a half hour, the men have hoisted their bloody prizes and disappeared into the bush.

The ninth elephant, a baby only a few months old and the sole witness to the brutal event, stands vigilantly by its mother's body, waiting for her to revive. The baby's patience and faith are long—too long. Unable to feed and care for himself, the infant will slowly starve, still hoping for his mother, aunts, and cousins to awake. Or, more likely, hyenas or other predators will find it first.

Scenes of killing in the African bush are nothing new. Death, after all, has been part of the cycle of life there as long as both prey and predator have roamed the continent's vast plains and woodlands. What is new—and shocking—about the fictive scenario above is the frequency and utter wastefulness with which such killings have been enacted. Conservationists estimate that in the 1980s more than two hundred elephants

Opposite page: The elephant's tusks probably developed long ages ago as an implement to make feeding easier. Today the trunk is perfectly adequate for most aspects of feeding, and the elephant's tusks, coveted by humankind to create ivory ornaments, are simply a curse that has brought untold destruction to its kind.

died at the hands of poachers each day, reducing Africa's already dwindled elephant numbers by more than 50 percent. The single goal of these poachers has been to acquire the animal's ivory tusks. Once the ivory has been extracted, the corpses of these supremely sensitive, intelligent animals are left to rot without a thought given to the potential usefulness of the animals' skins and meat, or, more importantly, to the havoc the wholesale slaughter of elephants may be having upon the fragile environments and economies of Africa's developing nations.

With a day's haul of ivory representing an average year's wages to many Africans—and with consumers in Asia, Europe, and the United States mostly unaware, until recently, of ivory's bloody origins—it has been all too easy for humans to distance themselves from the great chain of life of which both they and the elephant are a part. It might be said, without oversimplifying the case too greatly, that the elephant's days have been numbered since the inception of the world's present consumer-driven economic and social structure. And certainly, for many people involved in protecting the African elephant, the great beasts' plight (and that of the Asian elephant as well) has come to represent a larger conflict, well developed in the industrialized nations and increasingly evident at the end of the twentieth century in the Third World, as rain forests vanish and human populations boom. This conflict between human needs and the needs of a healthy Mother Earth has been growing for a long time, and in the case of the elephant its roots stretch to antiquity, to the very beginnings of the ivory trade.

WHITE GOLD: A HISTORY OF CIVILIZATION'S QUEST FOR IVORY

As long as humans have had the leisure and inclination to carve, hunters have set out in pursuit of elephants' tusks. The luminous, cross-hatched texture of ivory has few peers for beauty, durability, and the ease with which it can be worked in fine detail. Because both males and females bear large tusks, and because their tusks are larger than those of their male Asian cousins, the African elephant has most often been the object of the ivory hunt. (Carvers in India, in fact, have been importing East African elephant tusks to supplement their own supplies for at least two thousand years.)

A group of rings and combs worked in Egypt about six thousand years ago, probably from tusks collected from North African animals, is usually considered the earliest confirmed use of the elephant's ivory in carvings. But some far more primitive European figures carved some twenty thousand years ago from mammoth ivory may more realistically reflect the ancient roots of this human tradition. In the early tenth century B.C., the Hebrew monarch Solomon's ivory throne became a fabled symbol of wisdom and power. In fact, writes E. E. Moore in *Ivory: Scourge of Africa* (1931):

> *Thrones of ivory stretch across the ages, for there is the . . . ivory throne sent by Hezekiah, King of Judah, as tribute to Sennacherib, the throne of ivory sent to the Etruscan King, Porsenna, and the ivory throne sent from Travancore by its Indian Prince to his Empress, Victoria of Britain. Perhaps we should include the ivory chair, inlaid with gold, of Suleiman the Magnificent, in which he sat while, on the feast of Bairam, all the harem women came to kiss the unspeakable Turkish foot.*

Although we know very little about the ivory trade of earliest times, apparently the kingdoms of the ancient world developed a strong appetite for objects made from the elephant's precious tusks. The pursuit of ivory for trade, coupled with the capture of countless animals for use in numerous Roman spectacles, decimated the North African elephant population by about the seventh century A.D. Thereafter, the flow of ivory from Africa to Europe, where the substance was particularly in demand for use in religious screens and tryptichs, and the East slowed to a trickle until about the seventeenth century.

Predating this early ivory trade, tribal peoples had for countless ages hunted elephants on a small scale using spears, bows with poisoned arrows, pitfall traps, or a method known as hamstringing, which involved slashing the leg tendons and waiting for the animal to weaken from loss of blood. Elephants were a source of rich fat, almost nonexistent in many of the game animals that formed the basis of some traditional African diets. Killing an elephant by these methods was a time-consuming process. Simply finding the prey could take many hours and, once the animal was wounded, the hunter then might have to continue tracking it, now crazed with pain and considerably more dangerous, for several days before death finally occurred. Because the hunt was so arduous, these tribesmen tended to take only as many animals as their communities needed to maintain health, again leaving the elephant population relatively undisturbed. The balance finally shifted with the reemergence of a genuine ivory lust and the development of firearms whose bullets, properly placed, could stop an elephant in its tracks.

In the 1600s the nations of Europe were enjoying their first competitive bloom as world trade powers. The west coast of Africa became an

Northwind Picture Archives

Pitfalls were often used by traditional African hunters to trap elephants. An elephant kill meant a feast of meat and a surplus of fat, and most parts of the animal were utilized by the hunters.

important focus for European traders as their countrymen began to demand cheap labor for their expanding empires. Along with the West African slave trade came a renewed interest in ivory, and elephants began to be hunted more extensively. As long as only a few wealthy and powerful individuals could afford objects made of costly materials such as ivory, and indigenous peoples sought elephants only occasionally for food, African elephants as a species were relatively safe. But with the advent of European colonialism and, following on its heels, the Industrial Revolution, much larger numbers of people than ever before could afford luxury items made from ivory—and there was the means to produce them on a mass scale. Whereas before ivory had been used mainly for ritual items or small personal adornments, the objects produced from the precious tusks soon came to include everyday items such as rosary beads, pistol grips, fittings for lutes and other musical instruments, dice, toothpicks, prayer wheels, fly whisks, mah-jongg tiles, chopsticks, and many considerably less tasteful or useful *objets*.

Ivory lust intensified and persisted into the nineteenth century. As the North and West African elephant herds shrank, much of the trade shifted to the east coast of Africa, where British, Portuguese, and German hunters expanded the traditional Arab trade routes into the interior in search of ever more ivory. Getting the ivory out of the interior had never been easy, and this new phase of the trade saw a continuation of the brutalities begun on the west coast. Traders who needed porters for the heavy tusks terrorized African villages when they did not receive the cooperation they desired. They also forced the inhabitants into slavery in order to haul the ivory overland to the coast ports, disrupting the traditional relationships between Africans and wildlife and setting in motion a process of change that continues to this day. In southern Africa, too, European ivory hunters and land-hungry Boer settlers all but exterminated the elephant during this period. Between 1850 and 1890, in fact, an estimated forty-seven thousand elephants reportedly were killed each year to supply just the London market with ivory—and there were many other centers devoted to the commodity. Although Africans do not seem to have collected large amounts of ivory during most of their long history, toward the end of this period the feudal rulers of Buganda and Bunyoro, two Ugandan kingdoms, began to accumulate stockpiles of the precious material, perhaps in response to the feverish acquisitions of European traders.

With slaughter on such a large scale, by 1920, the majestic creatures that from time immemorial numbered many tens of millions had been reduced to remnant herds totaling only about one million individuals. Recognizing that the slaughter was perhaps getting out of hand, the colonial authorities instituted a licensing system for elephant hunting

In the early days of European ivory hunting, only tusks from large bulls, such as this pair weighing 120 pounds (54 kg), were taken. Today, mature bulls are so scarce that poachers kill any animal with tusks, even youngsters bearing ivory weighing only 7 or 8 pounds (3.1 or 3.6 kg).

© FPG International

In the late nineteenth century and the early years of the twentieth, every sport hunter had to have his elephant—or perhaps a hundred. As a result, before 1900, the elephant had been exterminated in southern Africa.

in East Africa. World War I provided a distraction from ivory hunting, as both European colonists and Africans left home to join in the fighting. After the war, ivory hunters found the practice of their profession more and more difficult, as colony after African colony ceased issuing unlimited elephant hunting licenses. Nevertheless, the live-it-up years of the 1920s saw two new uses for ivory, primarily in the United States: the annual production of at least sixty thousand billiard balls and of many hundreds of thousands of piano keys. The professional hunters continued trying to meet the demand by hunting where they still were allowed—in the Belgian Congo, Uganda, Sudan, and the Oubangi Province of French Equatorial Africa. By 1929, the last holdout among these territories, Oubangi, also stopped issuing its unlimited elephant licenses. As if in accord, the Depression arrived, deflated the demand for ivory, and gave the elephants an additional opportunity to recover their numbers.

The years following World War II saw the development of plastic replacements for many items previously made from ivory (though demand for the real thing began to grow once again, no doubt encouraged by the postwar economic boom). These years saw increasing agitation against colonial rule as well and, eventually, the emergence of independent African nations. Balancing urgent needs for education, health care, and economic development against limited resources, many of these new nations inherited national parks systems and conservation attitudes formulated in the days of colonialism. Some countries such as Kenya and Tanzania have, in the almost thirty years since their independence, protected elephants as best they could within this inherited infrastructure that was quite foresighted for its time. A few nations, notably Zimbabwe and Botswana, have looked carefully at their land-use and other economic requirements and struck out in innovative new conservation directions, with an encouraging degree of success. Other countries, such as Mozambique, Uganda, and Zambia, have been so beset with political and economic strife that conservation—whether of elephants or of other species—may simply have fallen to the bottom of their lists of national priorities.

ENTER THE POACHER

At the heart of Africa's elephant crisis is the fact that the continent's resources for conservation have been stretched far beyond their effective limits. The result has been that in spite of strong international controls on the ivory trade, rampant poaching in the last decade has reduced the continent's elephant population to the lowest and most alarming levels yet reported. In 1979, approximately 1.3 million elephants still romped about the grasslands and forests of Africa; at the end of 1989, their numbers were estimated at 625,000, perhaps fewer. The destruction has been uneven: Some stable countries that have carefully managed their wildlife have an overabundance of elephants, while others, either less attentive or plagued with civil conflicts, have suffered severe losses ranging from up to 50 percent of their herds to virtual extinction. Regardless of the occasional optimistic local situation, experts agree that with a continent-wide population of about 600,000, the danger of extinction for the elephant is extremely high (see "The African Elephant: Poaching and the Road to Extinction," page 32).

In many cases, official corruption has played a strong part in the elephant's demise. To cite just one disparity, Kenya reported ivory exports of 55 tons (49.5 metric tons) in 1976, while the traders of a single ivory center, Hong Kong, reported imports from Kenya of 235 tons (211.5 metric tons). By far the strongest factors, though, have been the increasing demand for ivory that started in the 1970s, when tusks began to be bought and sold as a commodity much like gold, and the lack of effective deterrents against poaching; throughout the 1980s poaching accounted for approximately 80 percent of the ivory traded worldwide. Also, post-independence unrest in many African countries has made automatic weapons such as M-14s, G3s, and AK-47s widely available to poachers throughout the continent, greatly accelerating the rate of slaughter. With cash hard to come by among rural Africans and inflation putting the squeeze on urbanites, the combination of these factors has made poaching and the illegal ivory trade an irresistible avocation for many people.

The poacher could not be successful without a dependable market. Hong Kong, with about three thousand people employed in the trading, retailing, and carving of tusks, has long been the world center for the

F.S. Mitchell/Tom Stack & Associates

Poaching in the late twentieth century has been ruthless, quick, and efficient. Automatic weapons have made the killing easy; chainsaws and other equipment have made the extraction of ivory and a fast getaway almost a given.

ivory trade, the marketplace through which most ivory—legal and illegal—passed before being channeled on to its ultimate consumers. Lesser trading centers have included Singapore, Dubai, the United Arab Emirates, and the small African nation Burundi, which has no elephants within its borders, but has long reigned as Africa's largest exporter.

In recent years Japan, the economic superpower of the 1980s, became the largest ivory consumer; this tiny country imported about 40 percent of the world's available tusks during the past decade, and supports its own extensive carving industry. The Japanese, like their predecessors in ivory consumption, have demanded ever more ivory as their wealth has increased. Similarly, their local craftsmen also convert the elephant's pride and glory into items, such as *hanko* (personalized name seals used instead of signatures on documents), or *netsukes* (small figures of animals or plants which adorn kimonos) that could easily be carved from other materials if not for the centuries-old prestige associated with owning ivory-made objects. The United States and Europe fell behind somewhat in their demand for ivory, but together they imported about 33 percent of the world's total during the 1980s, mostly in worked forms such as jewelry.

A treaty called the Convention on International Trade in Endangered Species of Wild Flora and Fauna (CITES—pronounced ''sigh-tease'') has played the strongest role in regulating the ivory trade to control poaching. The Asian elephant, which numbers between twenty-nine thousand and forty-four thousand in the wild, has been listed for many years on

During the 1980s, African elephants were slaughtered every day. Beginning in 1989, a total international ban on the ivory trade among **CITES** members has substantially slowed the killing.

© Robert Visser

A craftsman in Arusha, Tanzania, puts the finishing touches on a carved tusk prior to the **CITES** ban. Even before the ban, ivory carving provided only a very small amount of income for most African nations.

Appendix I of the CITES treaty. This classes an animal as truly endangered, prohibiting all commercial trade in the species among CITES signatory nations. Appendix II, where the African elephant was listed until late 1989, signifies that a species is threatened. With this status, limited trade was allowed through a system of permits and quotas that, theoretically, should have kept materials obtained through poaching off the market. Because CITES signatories can refuse to follow the convention's regulations, and since several nations have not ratified the treaty, a number of loopholes existed that helped perpetuate the trade in poached ivory. By the mid-1980s, both conservationists and researchers in the field, alarmed, were organizing to have CITES transfer the African elephant to Appendix I, and their concern began to stir action in other areas.

In September 1988 the conservation atmosphere began heating up in Kenya (along with Tanzania, hard hit by poachers and highly visible because of its strong tourist industry). Kenyan paleontologist Richard Leakey accused the country's minister of tourism of failing to move against game park officials suspected of collaborating with poachers. He also charged that the figure of twenty-two thousand elephants in Kenya—compared to the sixty-five thousand counted in 1979—was inaccurate, that the figure covered up the fact that recent spates of poaching had reduced the population to no more than nineteen thousand. Soon afterward, Kenya moved to strengthen its antipoaching efforts by giving rangers permission to shoot to kill when coping with poachers; in April 1989 the country followed up with the appointment of the outspoken Dr. Leakey, who had been running the national museums, as director of the government's Department of Wildlife and Conservation Management.

One of Leakey's first acts in his new post was to preside, with Kenyan President Daniel T. arap Moi, over the public burning of 13 tons (11.7 metric tons) of ivory confiscated by the government from poachers. The $3.6 million the ivory would have brought in a sale was to have been applied to refurbishing the sorely under-equipped game parks, which had been functioning since the late 1970s on a shoestring budget provided by Parliament through the central treasury. Leakey and Moi chose instead the dramatic gesture of burning the ivory as a way to focus international attention on the poaching problem and demonstrate the depth of Kenya's commitment to stamping out official corruption and saving its elephants.

Leakey then proceeded with a series of sweeping changes in his new bailiwick, including the already-planned reorganization of the country's game parks as a parastatal agency, Kenya Wildlife Services, with the goal of turning a profit. With better accountability and direct access to funds generated by tourism, the parks set about upgrading equipment and salaries, arming rangers with automatic weapons, training them for antipoaching patrols, and releasing funds to reward poaching informants. Leakey also announced his intention of raising an ambitious $200 million from the international economic community to repair and modernize Kenya's parks and reserves and to institute new wildlife management techniques, including profit sharing between conservation areas and local residents, and fencing certain conflicted park borders. Corrupt and ineffectual park employees were also investigated and dismissed. Results under the Leakey plan were almost immediate: After a year under his management, park rangers had killed at least one hundred poachers and the loss of elephants had slowed to one hundred per year rather than the one thousand per year of 1988 and earlier. In 1990, the country lost only about thirty elephants, many of these to causes other than poaching.

Tanzania, too, was galvanized into action on behalf of its elephants. Following the implication of a Tanzanian member of parliament, a journalist, a Catholic priest, and several diplomats (including an ambassador) in the trade and shipment of illegal ivory, the government launched Operation Uhai (after the Swahili for *life*) in June 1989. In Uhai's first four months, the combined forces of Tanzania's police, army, and wildlife departments arrested close to two thousand people and seized large quantities of tusks. With the risk of incarceration and fines no longer a mere threat, other Tanzanian poachers quickly got rid of their ivory rather than be caught in Uhai's expanding net. Like Kenya, Tanzania lost about 70 percent of its 316,000 elephants during the 1980s; unfortunately, Tanzania's economy, including the tourism sector, isn't nearly as healthy as its neighbor's, but there may still be time to salvage a future for the 85,000 elephants that remained in 1989.

Although the great majority of Africa's elephants live outside Kenya and Tanzania, these countries' responses seemed to symbolize the entire continent's willingness to confront the loss of its elephants and turn the process around. Outside Africa, action on behalf of the elephant grew equally dramatic. In May 1989 Sotheby's, the internationally renowned auction house, acknowledged the severity of the poaching problem when it withdrew two pairs of uncarved African elephant tusks from a planned sale and promised to stop dealing in ivory less than fifty years old. A group of prominent American designers—among them Bill Blass, Liz Claiborne, and Oscar de la Renta—denounced the past and future use of ivory in high fashion. In the summer of 1989 a number of nations—among them the United States, Canada, Australia, the twelve nations of the European Community, Hong Kong, Japan, Switzerland, Taiwan, and the United Arab Emirates—unilaterally banned ivory imports in anticipation of a change in the African elephant's CITES listing. At one point, a major story on elephants seemed to appear in the international media every day. Finally, with public awareness at an all-time high, in October 1989 representatives of the 103 CITES nations met in Switzerland and upgraded the African elephant to endangered status with a listing on Appendix I and a total ban on the international ivory trade set for January 18, 1990.

The CITES decision has been far from universally popular, although certain countries, particularly Japan, that might have been expected to circumvent the ban fell into line with little objection. Interestingly, Cynthia Moss, director of the Amboseli Elephant Project in Kenya, sees Japan's compliance as an outgrowth of the country's growing awareness of its role as a world power: "In the few months before the CITES decision there was a great deal of interest in elephants suddenly, and I had three Japanese film crews come down to Amboseli. . . . While these people were doing their interviews, you could just feel that they were very embarrassed, that they were afraid they were going to be held up to ridicule once more in the same way that they were with the whales, and that they just didn't want another situation like that on their hands."

However, Zimbabwe, Botswana, and South Africa, nations whose elephant populations had been increasing through effective manage-

The few African art markets with a strong trade in ivory goods, such as this one in Dakar, Senegal, catered mainly to tourists. The largest centers by far for the carving industry have traditionally been located in Hong Kong, Tokyo, and other Asian cities.

ment strategies, objected to the CITES ban. These countries maintained that the decision was unfair because it assisted only those nations who had not cared responsibly for their elephants, and it would deprive their own better-managed wildlife departments of important foreign exchange earned through the legal sale of culled ivory. In addition, Mozambique and Angola, whose elephant populations are considerably less hefty, also opposed the CITES decision, probably because the ivory trade had been quietly providing a major source of funding for their countries' civil wars.

In some circles the fear was that instead of halting poaching by cutting demand and prices, a ban might drive the illegal ivory trade further underground and consequently, further beyond the control of enforcement authorities. So far this does not seem to have happened, but Britain muddied the waters when it granted Hong Kong a six-month grace period before compliance with the ban to enable its traders to sell off the huge stockpiles of tusks they had accumulated in case of such an eventuality. Immediately following the British announcement in January 1990, a new round of poaching broke out in Kenya's Tsavo National Park, one of the hardest-hit areas in the 1980s. "No doubt about it, there was a connection," says Bill Woodley, the warden in charge of antipoaching operations at Tsavo. "It had been quiet for months, and then we found ten dead elephants all at once." This new wave of poaching, before it was brought under control, resulted in the loss of fifty-seven elephants; this was particularly disturbing since poaching losses for the entire country during all of 1989 amounted to only about one hundred animals. Conservationists had predicted this reaction from poachers unless a *total* trade ban was effected; their fears were intensified when Hong Kong traders began suggesting that their grace period be extended until the next meeting of the CITES secretariat, scheduled for Tokyo in 1992.

By the beginning of 1991—though the situation must be monitored day-by-day—the ban appeared largely effective in spite of the continued international quibbling. The United Arab Emirates had returned to the CITES fold after a two-year absence, and even such a notably recalcitrant country as Somalia—a desperately poor nation through which many of the ethnic Somali poachers plaguing Kenya had been funneling illegal tusks—had decided to go along with the CITES ban. The ban seemed to have had the desired effect of dampening ivory prices: According to the Kenyan *Daily Nation*, tusks that had been selling on the black market for $66 to $88 per pound ($30 to $40 per kg) before the ban were down to $4.50 to $6.50 per pound ($2 to $3 per kg) just four months after it was enacted—too little to be worth much risk for poachers, whose profits would be a fraction of these amounts. Reports indicated that retail sales were also depressed in Europe, the United States, and Hong Kong, and prices for the little stock that was moving had dropped startlingly.

It is still too soon to know whether the CITES ban will mean more than a temporary lull in ivory poaching, and there are still ugly signs that ivory lust continues to burn unabated, if subterraneanly, in spite of the apparent downturn in the market. India, which has consistently toed the hard line against imports of illegal ivory from Africa, briefly experimented with the use of mammoth ivory (as have other countries; picking up mammoth ivory was an alternative source of income for Russian fishermen over the past few centuries when the fish weren't running) in its domestic carving industry during the mid-1980s. Taking up India's cue, a group of Japanese ivory traders visited the Soviet Union early in 1990 to investigate the feasibility of retrieving large amounts of ivory from corpses of the extinct woolly mammoth, frozen under the Siberian tundra for ten thousand years. Despite the fact that mammoth ivory is mottled with dark streaks and harder to carve than elephant ivory, the price for such tusks had already rocketed to $2,200 per pound ($1,000 per kg) by midyear.

Sadly, the pressure that had with great effort been diverted from the beleaguered elephant has quietly been transferred to another creature with tusks. During 1989, poachers in speedboats shot for their ivory at least twelve thousand Alaskan walruses, whose tusks can grow up to 3 feet long (.9 m) and weigh 8 pounds (3.6 kg), in the waters of the Bering Strait. Headless corpses riddled with bullet holes washed up on Siberian and Alaskan beaches by the hundreds, accompanied by others, still intact, from which the poachers were unable to remove the ivory before the butchered animals were claimed by the sea. The carnage is strongly reminiscent of African scenes in the last decade.

As with the elephant and certain African tribes, the walrus is still an important staple of the indigenous Eskimos of Siberia and Alaska. The Eskimos traditionally hunted walruses with kayaks and harpoons and are still permitted by United States law to take as many animals as is necessary for food and clothing. With the price of walrus ivory soaring, not only Eskimos (many of whom still subsist outside the mainstream American economy) have turned to poaching as a source of quick cash and even drugs from Far Eastern traders who have set up shop in Alaska. Like African elephants, Alaska's 230,000 remaining walruses face the very real possibility of extinction by the end of the century. This wanton poaching of walruses serves as a warning that conservationists and governments have not managed to eliminate the taste for ivory through education and publicity, and that poaching pressure could be redirected toward elephants at any time.

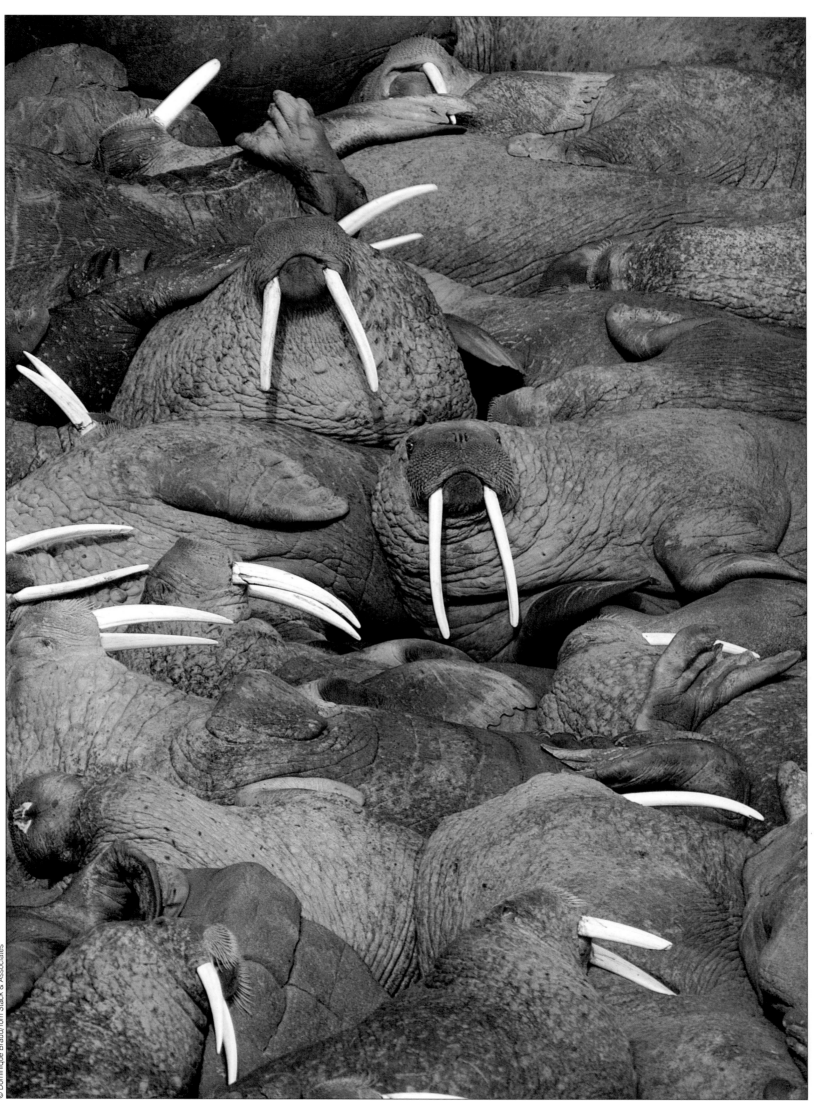

LIVING WITH ELEPHANTS

Some conservationists worry that all the publicity surrounding the antipoaching drive may have obscured the real problem the African elephant faces. Even if the CITES ban is effective beyond all expectations, and the elephants are able to recover their numbers, a less easily managed conflict awaits all Africa's wildlife: a rapidly growing human population and too little land for both people and animals.

Kenya's population, for instance, is increasing at a rate approaching 4 percent each year, and most African nations fall in with rates not far below. Kenya, like much of Africa, has a high proportion of nonarable land, and it has set aside extremely generous tracts as game parks and wildlife reserves (Tsavo National Park, for example, is approximately the size of Israel and three times the size of Yellowstone National Park in the United States). In spite of some success with family planning in a culture that values children as wealth, Kenya's population is expected to double not once, but twice in the near future. As it does so, the demands made upon viable land by both people and animals are likely to become quite intense, as they already are in Asia. (Under such conditions, the fact that politically stable Kenya has experienced one of the

The poaching problem may have been solved for now, but elephants and humans are increasingly competing for the same land, a conflict that will be far more difficult to address.

continent's most extensive poaching problems may not be coincidental.)

With so many young mouths to feed, finding space on the continent for both agriculture and elephants will be difficult indeed. Few creatures must be less compatible with agricultural development than the elephant, which has a great fondness for specific foods and the intelligence to return year after year to sites where it can obtain them. This characteristic, along with the seasonal availability of water and forage in certain areas, means that, in following traditional migratory routes established over centuries, elephants often stray from reserves and game parks onto private lands now devoted to agriculture. A medium-size herd passing through a mango grove will almost surely destroy both fruit and trees with the efficiency of a cyclone. Likewise, even a single elephant free-ranging overnight in a maize field or small tea plantation can spell instant economic ruin for a family struggling to make ends meet on the equivalent of $400 or less a year. Faced with such a prospect, few farmers would hesitate to fell a trespassing elephant.

Unless Kenyans and other African peoples find strong incentives for preserving their wild heritage, there will be very little the international conservation community can do to help save it. Tiny Rwanda, the site of Dian Fossey's mountain gorilla studies and one of the world's most densely populated countries, provides an example. In the early 1980s the competition in Rwanda for farmland for people and grazing land for elephants grew so urgent that its government dealt with the problem by airlifting (at great cost) a few elephants into a secure park and simply shooting the rest. Today, Rwanda is home to only about seventy elephants. Without strong economic advantages associated with conservation, there will be nothing to keep other countries' elephant populations from going the way of Rwanda's—or the way of the American bison, for that matter.

There is more than one way to feed a family, however, and several African countries have, fortunately, dealt with the undesirable aspects of hosting elephants with more creativity than Rwanda. South Africa's solution, heralded recently in *The New York Times* as the conservation wave of the future, has been a combination of fencing and culling. Kruger National Park is always home to seven thousand elephants, give or take only a few. If the elephants increase in number beyond that level, they threaten not only their own food and water supply, but that of the other species in the completely enclosed park. When this happens, rangers shoot as many elephants as necessary to bring them back to the seven-thousand mark. The animals are then processed and the various products—ivory, meat, skin, bone meal, trophies, hair—are sold. The monies, along with the fees paid by visitors to the park, are returned to conservation programs.

© Gerry Ellis/The Wildlife Collection

In Rwanda, where the human population is unusually dense and arable land particularly scarce, the government has already decided that numerous elephants are a luxury the country cannot afford.

Esthetically, the South African approach presents a problem, since the element of wildness has been removed from Kruger; its elephants essentially have the run of an extremely large and well-run zoo. Conservationists also warn that fencing such a large area may be dangerous ecologically. A single park might successfully get away with such a practice for a number of years, but they say fencing on a large scale across all of Africa could lead to massive desertification of fragile lands. The reason for this is that fencing prevents the ancient regeneration process facilitated by the seasonal migrations and bush clearing of elephant herds from occurring.

Other scientists point out that elephant physiology provides natural checks and balances to ensure against overpopulation, such as a rise in the age at which elephants reach puberty, and a lengthening of the interval between calves when conditions are less than optimal. Culling prevents the operation of these natural controls and may unnaturally stimulate the birth rate, by making the food supply seem larger than it actually is, when environmental conditions ordinarily would cause births to taper off. An example often cited in opposition to culling is a period in the 1970s at Kenya's Tsavo National Park when the elephant population had increased greatly, and the animals seemed to be destroying many of the trees in the park. An unexpected drought that killed thousands of elephants interrupted the debate on whether to cull or not. Had the animals been culled, opponents argued, the elephant population would have been seriously endangered when the drought struck and killed additional animals.

There is a good case against culling on moral grounds as well. As Cynthia Moss eloquently states the case: "Elephants are extremely intelligent, long-lived, complex mammals. Those who would cull them as a solution to conservation problems often say such operations are not disruptive because whole families are killed, and when there are no survivors, the other elephants don't know what is going on. But the other elephants *do* know what's happening. They can hear sounds from vast distances, they find the bones of dead elephants, they can smell their blood.

"From our data we know the families aren't always together. You could go in one day and kill what you think is a family of ten elephants, but it may be that five of the family were off somewhere else that day. And individual families have ties to other families that may extend back over several generations. Imagine their distress even if they simply believed a family gone—imagine how human families would feel if they lived under this stress from day to day."

But even with the strong respect she has for elephants, Moss concedes that some compromise may be necessary. "I am not against hunting of older animals, although I think it will be thirty to fifty years before Kenya can get enough of its male elephants up to older age classes to permit this," she says. "But it's not right to cull elephants—it's not moral. We simply know too much about their concept of death and their long bonds."

The wisest approach of all, perhaps, may be the very successful policies implemented by countries like Zimbabwe and Botswana, a version of so-called sustainable development that is compatible with the needs of land, elephants, and humans. As practiced in Zimbabwe, sustainable development combines agriculture, tourism, and conservation, leaving the decision making about wild animals, including the endangered ele-

© Gerry Ellis/The Wildlife Collection

phant, up to the local people. With this kind of policy, farmers are given control of any wild animals that happen onto their property. If elephants destroy crops, the farmer is free to kill the animals and make any use of them that he wishes, including the sale of their ivory, meat, and skin. On the other hand, the farmer and his neighbors might choose to cultivate the elephants' presence, even to the extent of abandoning their crops, because he can offer very profitable sport hunting or photo safaris to tourists. Either way, the economic pressure from wildlife is relieved, and many farmers are finding that the elephants can often be more lucrative alive than dead, bringing back tourists year after year instead of yielding only a quick, one-time profit. Since they stand to

The key to future elephant conservation seems to lie in finding ways to make the animals more valuable to the people who live in closest proximity to them.

benefit from the elephants' presence, the local people are also on guard against poachers and report any untoward activities to the wildlife department.

In Botswana, much the same principle is at work in its carefully controlled sport hunting program. Tourists can take a limited number of older animals each year—for a handsome price. Sport hunting provides much-needed employment opportunities for Botswanan trackers and safari workers, and the presence of hunters in the bush helps deter poaching.

Both Zimbabwe and Botswana are in the fortunate position of having flourishing elephant herds. Botswana's elephants have more than doubled in number since 1979, to 51,000, and Zimbabwe had a healthy 43,000 at last count. Rather unfairly, these countries have paid a price for bucking the continent-wide trend. The CITES trade ban that has helped slow poaching in other African countries effectively denies their people a market for culled ivory, and officially prevents most foreign hunters from taking trophies home from Botswana and Zimbabwe; this makes the sport less attractive for some, and perhaps steers them to other hunting grounds.

Still, some type of sustainable development may hold out the best hope for long-term survival of Africa's elephants. Zambia, which has suffered catastrophic losses to poachers from among its famous Luangwa Valley elephants, recently implemented a program, the Luangwa Valley Resource Development Project, modeled on Zimbabwe's wildlife policies, which has met with enthusiasm from the local people. Also, in May 1990 Kenya sponsored an international conference to explore options such as sustainable development and profit sharing. One of the best-known examples of the latter is the longstanding cooperation between Kenya's Amboseli National Park and the Masai herdsmen who live along its boundaries.

The profit sharing between Amboseli and the local pastoralists dates from the thirteen years directly following 1963, the year of independence. During these years Amboseli was officially a wildlife reserve in which animals were protected but humans also retained some limited rights. The reserve was under the control of a local governing body, the Kajiado County Council, which redistributed tourism profits from the reserve in the form of various community development projects for the Masai.

When the Kenyan government gazetted Amboseli as a national park in 1974, it struck a compromise agreement with the Kajiado County Council. In exchange for the Masai giving up grazing rights and other limited activities such as logging within the former reserve boundaries, the council would continue to receive all the revenues from tourist

Opposite page: Kenya's Amboseli National Park, home to one of the largest groups of elephants undisturbed by poaching in all of Africa, is located in the heart of a traditional grazing area of the pastoral Masai people.

Sustainable development is very much the watchword among African governments and wildlife officials today, not only in Masai land but in Zimbabwe, Zambia, and other countries. Once the local residents obtain a stake in the economic benefits of preserving elephants near their lands, the hope is that both people and animals will flourish.

lodges within the park and a percentage of all gate receipts. In addition, the park would provide a pipeline to divert water from an important dry season water supply within the park to areas outside its boundaries where the Masai cattle could drink without endangering wildlife habitats. The park would also pay grazing compensation for wild animals that drifted out of the park and onto Masai lands. Funds from the park would also pay for construction of a school, a community center, and medical facilities in the area. This innovative approach was made possible by the way the park evolved from previous commitments, and it should have made a significant contribution toward bettering the living conditions of the Masai, one of the Kenyan tribes least integrated into the modern life of the country.

Results, however, have been somewhat mixed, and the plan only now shows signs of one day working as it was intended to. The pipeline, when built, turned out to be too small to work effectively. Then, the park, operating on a shoestring budget during the 1980s ("barely enough," points out Cynthia Moss, "to buy a major part for the park's road-grading machine"), ran out of money to buy diesel to operate the pump. Kenyans around Amboseli and elsewhere have also found compensation for wildlife damage notoriously difficult to extract from the government authorities in charge of such programs.

© Gerald Corsi/Tom Stack & Associates

In spite of these broken promises, the Masai were still asked to toler-
ate incursions of wildlife onto their lands and to refrain from spearing
animals as part of the initiation of their *morani*, or warriors. When an
especially harsh drought hit the district in 1984, causing great suffering
and deaths among elephants and other wildlife, as well as Masai children and cattle, the park reversed policy; the Masai and their cattle were
allowed into the park for both food and water until the crisis passed.
But for a long time, says Moss, "We've had an old-fashioned conservation mentality here. In some ways it was 'them against us' or 'the park
against the people on the outside.'"

With the reorganization of the national parks and reserves under
Kenya Wildlife Services the future looks much brighter. The ill-fated
pipeline project is being reworked in a larger dimension. Moss says she
doesn't think that the park will get to the point again where they have
to worry about money. She says the parastatal has drastically changed
the whole situation and that Amboseli continues to make more money
than any other park in the entire system. Park entry fees for tourists
have more than doubled, and the Masai will receive an increased proportion of these fees, 25 percent. As Moss explains, "There are going to
be various committees involved and local district development officers.
But this money will be going to the group ranches around the park. It's

Education may be the key to making conservation work in Africa.
Westerners, with easy access to a variety of information, may
know far more about elephants than a child growing up in a
rural African district—a child who will one day help make crucial
decisions that affect the fate of the animal.

not as though the local people haven't benefitted from the park in many ways in the past, but the Kajiado County Council is a hundred miles (160 km) away, and not very much trickles back to the people right next to the park.

"We've got to do more for the people living in the areas around the wildlife preserves," Moss adds. "If we can't work out the situation with the Masai, we'll lose the park. That is the most important thing that has to be done in terms of Amboseli and in terms of Kenya as a whole."

James F. Dunn, agricultural development officer for the United States Agency for International Development (USAID) in Nairobi, Kenya, agrees: "It's going to be very, very difficult to manage the land-use conflict, particularly if Africans don't come to grips, somehow, with making wildlife more beneficial to people." The complexity of the task at hand is part of what motivated USAID to become involved once again in funding natural resources programs after years of concentrating mainly upon agricultural research. Most of USAID's wildlife-oriented resource projects in Kenya have education at their heart, whether interpretive centers established in national parks, training for wardens at U.S. universities or locally, or materials such as the coursebook for an adult literacy program developed jointly with the African Wildlife Foundation.

Education, Dunn believes, is the key to making conservation work in Africa. Westerners, with easy access to a variety of information, may know far more about elephants than a child growing up in a rural African district—a child who will one day help make crucial decisions that affect whether the elephant will live on in all its splendor, or eventually die out at civilization's hand. The Wildlife Clubs of Kenya (a school-based organization that functions somewhat like American 4-H clubs, with outings and projects designed around wildlife and natural-resources education) draws consistent praise for the work it has done with children. Unfortunately, the Wildlife Clubs are probably somewhat more effective in urban areas, where financial resources are concentrated, than in poorer, isolated rural areas most affected by wildlife.

Dunn also sees evidence that the educational effects of widespread press and the lobbying of international conservation organizations have begun to take hold among the people who currently make decisions about wildlife. "In Kenya," Dunn says, "wildlife has been exploited in the past, and at the very highest levels there seemed that there was no end to it. Now, it does appear, probably simply because of economics, that they recognize that they do have a very valuable resource and that they ought to try to manage it better. . . ."

There is also, Dunn notes, "an emerging sense that Kenya has been looking at wildlife in a very narrow sense—that is, in terms of tourism

© Gerald Corsi/Tom Stack & Associates

only. And there are many opportunities to capitalize on wildlife. The
southern African states seem to be much farther ahead on that. So
there's a recognition in Kenya that they need to look at a lot of other
things—everything from skins to meat to opening up new areas and
kinds of tourism."

Indeed, there is a new take-charge attitude in Kenya regarding wildlife
management that echoes the assertiveness of its neighbors to the south.
This may derive, in part, from worries that the realignment of power in
Eastern Europe may divert Western aid funds to this new area for development and a growing sense that, more than ever, Africa needs to begin
standing on its own feet. Richard Leakey set a precedent in the May
1990 meeting he called to discuss Kenya Wildlife Services' ten-year plan
with the international aid agencies and conservation organizations from
whom he hopes to raise approximately $200 million in funding. At the
meeting, he asked his audience to examine the proposal and look for
ways they felt their organizations could participate within its frame-
work. This, Leakey explained, would be far more effective in the long
term than having each organization add a pet project to what, in the
past, had often been an uncoordinated patchwork of efforts with dupli-
cations, unfortunate omissions, and some simply impracticable projects.

**African governments, having watched a precious resource dwindle,
realize more than ever the importance of protecting the elephant
to safeguard the tourist industry.**

Opposite page: The interaction between man and elephant over the millenia has been extremely rich. Surely our children deserve the pleasure and wonder of growing up knowing that such awe-inspiring creatures still roam free.

The goal—and the payoff for their participation—would be an independent, self-supporting Kenya Wildlife Services in the early years of the twenty-first century. "There may be those of you who think our plan is ambitious," Leakey declared. "But so is getting Kenya out of the Third World."

Before the concern about the greenhouse effect and global warming, tying the elephant's survival so closely to the future economic development of Africa, and to the principles of consumerism practiced in more developed parts of the world, might have seemed far-fetched. Today, however, few ethologists, conservationists, or government officials would dispute the intimate connection between the two, as we continue to learn more about the fragility and necessary balance of our precious Earth.

Saving the mighty African elephant from an impoverished, unnatural existence in zoos and a few parks may one day depend upon such high-tech solutions as genetic analysis of ivory, which could make it possible to determine the geographic origins of individual tusks and whether they were poached or legally harvested. But for now the answer seems to lie with plain, old-fashioned sacrifice—mainly from the people who live closest to these majestic creatures. Their sacrifices will be of convenience and, often, short-term prosperity, which we of the industrialized world have been unwilling to deny ourselves in the past. Likewise, thousands of Far Easterners have been asked not only to give up their jobs in the ivory-carving industry, but a time-honored tradition with ancient roots in their cultures, for the sake of these rare and wonderful creatures. Most of these concessions will be made in part for the people of the West, who have few wild places left, and realize increasingly that the earth's survival may depend upon preserving those that remain. Because the elephant's survival ultimately will benefit all of the world's citizens, it is only fair that Western consumers support local actions that defend the elephant, chiefly by resisting, until it is once again ecologically safe to do so, the vanity of buying and wearing ivory.

But perhaps the most important reason of all for saving the elephant, and one we may not begin to realize until it is too late, is contained in the words of Chief Seattle of the Nez Percé:

> *What happens to beasts will happen to man. All*
> *things are connected. If the great beasts are gone,*
> *man would surely die of a great loneliness of*
> *spirit.*

May all the world's people—and it will take all of us—find the wisdom and the determination to ensure that it will not be so.

Wardens on Patrol: Fighting Poachers on the Ground and from the Air

At the end of a long day on patrol, an African game warden searching for elephant poachers has often come upon such disheartening sights as this: another elephant gone forever, its ivory whisked away for a quick profit on the black market.

The Christen A-1 Husky taxis to a stop at the top of the dirt strip at Tsavo West National Park headquarters near Mtito Andei, Kenya. Soon the pilot, twenty-year-old Derek Rundgren, assistant warden, class one, receives permission to take off and pulls back the throttle. As the two-seater leaves the strip, a trio of ostriches strutting in the grass scatters in long-legged confusion while a smallish herd of twenty or thirty Cape buffalo startles, then careens away as the plane rises with a steady drone into the air. For Rundgren, great-nephew of a well-known white hunter, his first job has fulfilled two dreams. "I always wanted to fly in the bush, and I always wanted to join the game department," he says.

As the Husky gains altitude, the low bushes, newly green from the long rains, roll under the plane like the folds in a rich velvet mantle. Rundgren circles the strip and turns the plane toward the eastern sector of the park, where poaching has taken the heaviest toll on Tsavo's once abundant elephants. It's an hour or so after lunchtime, and the sun is past its zenith. Heat and the sound of the plane's engines soon fill the plane as Rundgren settles in for the second leg of his daily antipoaching patrol.

Because Rundgren is new to the job, he is still learning the park, a vast tract the size of Israel managed with the expertise of only 100 to 150 rangers, most on foot. He heads for an impressive formation, the Yatta Plateau, that cleaves Tsavo East like a backbone. The plateau is faced with rocky escarpments, a perfect setting, Rundgren explains, for poachers who like to track and trap elephants where they will be unable to run. Today's fly-by doesn't yield any new evidence of poaching, but beneath us we spot the weathered carcasses of fourteen elephants discovered almost a year ago, their bones scattered about a jutting triangular tip of the plateau in random clusters like a fortune-teller's sticks.

Rundgren presses on, following the Galana River, one of the permanent sources of water in the park, eager to cover more territory before evening. The sun is lower now, and the late-afternoon light flashing off the river makes distinguishing objects on the ground more difficult. Rundgren flies lower, at about 100 feet (30 m), to make up for the poor visibility; the reddish humps along the banks could be elephants tinted the bright hue of the park's soil from their dust baths, but up close they are only mounds of river clay. At this low altitude, Rundgren explains, he and his fellow pilots "look for vultures and evidence of poachers"—fires, abandoned hideouts, the armed men themselves.

Soon the Husky is climbing back to 400 feet (120 m), a better vantage point for spotting live elephants and elephant carcasses. Both types of observation are vital to Tsavo's antipoaching strategy, but with only three planes available, even alternating them doesn't give the wardens the kind of coverage they'd like. Each day the pilots decide together who will fly where, but their observation methods are their own. "It depends on your mood, really,"

says Rundgren with a grin. "If you're feeling cocky, you'll fly low." Knowing that army helicopter pilots are standing by at Voi, at the southern end of Tsavo East, as reinforcements should the wardens encounter weapons fire is somewhat reassuring, yet the danger these men in their light planes—and their colleagues on the ground—face each day remains very real nonetheless.

Recent changes in the way parks personnel are trained, including improved instruction in field craft, automatic weaponry, and military discipline, have sharpened the odds for rangers on patrol against poachers, says Bill Woodley, a former elephant hunter who began his career as a warden at Tsavo in 1948 and now directs antipoaching operations for both halves of the park. He notes with approval that recruitment of several hundred new Kenya Wildlife Services rangers, trained at the air force base at Magadi, has been heavy among young men of the "Masai, Samburu, and Turkana, tribes who are known for their knowledge of the bush—people who are tougher than the Somali poachers. The Somalis are a hard, desert people, and we'll need men who are as hard as they are to defeat them."

Another great help has been the institution of daily field allowances of 30 shillings ($1.50), paid to rangers who volunteer for night patrols, which can substantially increase the earnings of men who volunteer regularly. "The allowances have made a difference. Before, no one wanted to go out on night patrol," Woodley says. "It just wasn't worth the risk for the salary." Woodley hopes that the

Opposite page: Game wardens look forward to the time when elephants can regain their former personalities, when the memory of poaching is a distant one and the sight or scent of humans no longer causes them to run in panic.

influx of new recruits will boost the parks' force of rangers to around 250, a still inadequate number for the job at hand, but a distinct improvement.

A certain amount of monotony goes along with the danger associated with antipoaching work. On most patrols, nothing at all happens in the way of "contact," as Woodley and his wardens refer to encounters with poachers. But an active antipoaching presence may itself be one of the most important elements of protecting Tsavo's elephants. "With only three planes, there are occasions when all three are out for repairs," Woodley says. "And you can believe the poachers know when those times are."

As Rundgren turns the Husky back toward the headquarters at Mtito Andei, with some relief we conclude that his afternoon patrol is coming to an uneventful end. Although we've been in the air for more than three hours and the hum of the plane has taken on a comforting tone, we've seen only scattered buffalo, impala, fairly abundant herds of zebra, and several families of giraffe loping across the plain. As we cross from Tsavo East into Tsavo West, Rundgren spots our first elephant, a lone bull taking a leisurely drink from the edge of a water hole. Based on the observations from recent patrols, Woodley had concluded that most of the park's elephants had migrated into Tsavo West, which borders Tanzania, where they felt safer, and this spotting seems to confirm his conclusion. Farther on, we spot three families, one with eight members, one with eleven, and another with six. We circle the elephant families at medium altitude; they pay us no attention, and all seems well as we head once again for Mtito Andei and home.

As Rundgren noses the Husky down onto the runway, we bump past another quartet of elephants grazing drowsily beside the dirt strip used by their guardians in possibly the safest place in the park. "It's sad, what's happened to the elephants," Rundgren muses as he works through his post-flight checklist. "You want to do what you can, but it's difficult."

ELEPHANT WATCHING: WHERE TO GO

If reading about elephants has made you want to learn more, consider making these fascinating animals a focal point of your next long vacation or holiday. Here are some of the most likely countries for viewing elephants in or close to their natural habitats and, in brief, what sort of experience you can expect:

Africa

BOTSWANA

Along with Zimbabwe, its neighbor to the northeast, Botswana has gained a reputation for offering personalized safaris, partly because of the country's commitment to encouraging tourist development that sits lightly upon the land. Many camps are reachable only by small plane, and canoeing and walking safaris are common. Recommended for elephant watching are Moremi Wildlife Reserve, located within the hauntingly beautiful Okavango Delta, and Chobe National Park, with its huge elephant herds. Because Botswana's elephants remain largely untouched by poaching, they are perhaps more vocal and playful than many others on the continent. Write to Botswana Division of Tourism, Private Bag 0047, Gaborone, Botswana, for additional information.

KENYA

For those who have never traveled in Africa, Kenya is probably the place to wet your feet; this East African nation hopes to draw at least a million visitors each year during the 1990s. Kenya's elephant herds are not what they once were; most of the mature males have been killed for their ivory, but poaching has been brought under control. In spite of the professionalism grown of experience within the safari industry, some visitors lately have begun to complain that a visit to Kenya can sometimes be overpackaged—a frantic race to provide tourists with photographs of the Big Five game animals (including elephants) with little chance to simply experience the bush and the majestic surroundings. Ask questions to find a tour with a pace and focus that appeals to you. Kenyan national parks with elephant herds are among the world's most famous: Amboseli, Meru, Tsavo East and West, and Mount Elgon; also favored for elephant fanciers are two game reserves, Masai Mara and Samburu. Tourist information is available from the Kenya Office of Tourism, 424 Madison Avenue, New York, NY 10017; Doheny Plaza, Suite 111, 9100 Wilshire Boulevard, Beverly Hills, CA 90212; or 25 Brooks Mews, Davis Street, London W1Y 1LG.

NAMIBIA

Namibia, on the southwest coast of Africa, gained its independence from South Africa early in 1990. Huge elephant herds in the country's famous Etosha National Park migrate seasonally along the desert Etosha Pan and into Angola, to the north. Skeleton Coast National Park, named for the treacherous shoreline, is intriguing for its well-digging desert elephants, which were all but wiped out by poachers, but are now making a comeback. Namibia may well offer the most unusual backdrop for elephant watching on the entire continent. Further information on Namibia is available from SATOUR at the addresses given here.

SOUTH AFRICA

For those who like to travel without feeling they've left home, South Africa may be the most likely place

for elephant viewing. Kruger National Park, with some seven thousand elephants, is completely fenced and has paved game trails and a wide range of plush accommodations—it is undoubtedly the most developed park in Africa. The small Addo Elephant Park, with about one hundred elephants, represents an effort to preserve a species that was all but made extinct in the course of European settlement. In spite of these attractions, many people will continue to find a visit to South Africa unacceptable until apartheid is completely abolished. Further information is available from SATOUR (South Africa Tourist Corporation), 9465 Wilshire Boulevard, Beverly Hills, CA 90212; 307 North Michigan Avenue, Chicago, IL 60601; 747 Third Avenue, 20th floor, New York, NY 10018; or Regency House, 1-4 Warwick Street, London W1R 5WB.

TANZANIA

Kenya's neighbor to the south has suffered from a stagnant economy (and resulting weak infrastructure) that tends to make sight-seeing there a less soothing experience than in Kenya. Tanzania has four times as many elephants as Kenya in an area that is larger by about one half, and this may be enough of an attraction to make up for rough roads or other inconveniences. Parks to look into when planning a trip include: Lake Manyara National Park, Ngorongoro Conservation Area, Serengeti National Park, and the highly rated Tarangire National Park, all clustered around the tourist center of Arusha. Less known but with more substantial elephant populations are Selous Game Reserve and Ruaha National Park. For tourist information, write to Tanzania Tourist Corporation, 77 South Adley Street, London W1X 1HA.

ZAIRE

Virunga National Park, contiguous with the park of the same name in neighboring Rwanda and with Ruwenzori National Park in Uganda, is the place to see Africa's diminutive forest elephants. Virunga is a huge park in a huge country; to find elephants, head for either Rwindi or Vitshumbi. Rampant corruption and routine hassling of tourists are unfortunate aspects of this central African nation, and many tourists, with good reason, steer clear of Zaire. Hardier, more determined souls will find the lush jungle setting spectacular. Information is available from the Office National du Tourisme, Avenue des Orangiers 2A/2B, B.P. 9502, Kinshasa/Gombe, Zaire.

ZAMBIA

This southern African nation's staunch support (often including economic sanctions) of the region's many freedom movements, coupled with a disastrous fall in the prices of copper, the country's main mineral resource, has wreaked havoc with development plans over the years. Zambia is rich in wildlife, however, including dense elephant populations in North and South Luangwa national parks and Kafue National Park, and the country now sees tourism as its best bet for bringing needed hard currency into the economy. This piece of Livingstone country, still a little rough around the edges, probably isn't a good choice for a first visit to Africa, but for experienced travelers the unspoiled riches gathered along the Zambezi River may be a strong incentive to visit. Zambia's National Tourist Board will provide you with further details: 237 East 52nd Street, New York, NY 10022; or 2 Palace Gate, Kensington, London W8 5NF.

ZIMBABWE

While poachers were making free with Kenya and Tanzania's elephants during the 1980s, newly independent Zimbabwe was busy revising its tourist industry. Although the infrastructure in this southern African nation is not yet up to the level of, say, Kenya, it is catching up fast. Plentiful elephants, including large older males sporting huge tusks, in Hwange National Park, Matusadona National Park, and Gonarezhou ("the place of many elephants") National Park, are a powerful attraction, as are intimate canoeing and walking safaris. More information may be obtained from the Zimbabwe Tourist Office, 1270 Avenue of the Americas, Suite 1905, New York, NY 10020; or Colette House, 52-55 Picadilly, London W1V 9AA.

Asia

INDIA

India has been aggressively promoting tourism for the last few years, and a prime attraction is its wildlife, carefully protected since the 1960s, which in many cases has made a remarkable comeback. Several parks are of interest primarily for their elephants, particularly Periyar Wildlife Sanctuary in the south of the country. Also recommended for elephant watching are Corbett National Park in the north and Manas Wildlife Sanctuary and Kaziranga Wildlife Sanctuary (special permission required for entry) in the east. Elephants are also widely used for transport in most of India's other parks and for other types of tourist outings. Richly decorated elephants prepared for local festivals are much in evidence, and you can also see the elephant's image in architecture as decoration on the entrances to temples and other buildings. You can obtain more information from the Government of India Tourist Office, 30 Rockefeller Plaza, Suite 15, North Mezzanine, New York, NY 10112; 3550 Wilshire Boulevard, Suite 204, Los Angeles, CA 90010; or 7 Cork Street, London WIX 2AB.

NEPAL

Royal Chitwan National Park in Nepal, a fascinating country sandwiched between India and China, is known for its rebounding populations of tigers and one-horned Indian rhinoceroses, both of which were almost completely destroyed by poachers in the 1970s. Elephants are used to transport tourists on game treks and are an integral part of park visits. The elephant training camp nearby is open to visitors and offers a glimpse into the practice of an ancient tradition. Further information may be obtained from the Nepal Travel Bureau, 15 East 40th Street, Room 1204, New York, NY 10016.

THAILAND

This small Southeast Asian nation has about four thousand working elephants and as many remaining in the wild. In addition to Buddhist religious festivals, whose parades and processions may feature elephants, you may want to investigate daily tours offered by an active work and training camp located just north of the town of Chiang Mai. A two-day elephant-catching festival held each November in Surin gives the local Suay tribe a chance to exercise their traditional skills and is worth going out of your way to attend. Thailand also maintains a herd of royal white elephants. For more information contact the Thailand Tourist Office, 5 World Trade Center, Suite 2449, New York, NY 10048; 3440 Wilshire Boulevard, Suite 1101, Los Angeles, CA 90010; or 49 Albemarle Street, London WIX 3FE.

When planning an elephant watching trip to Asia or Africa, don't forget that seasonal rains often make the roads in many parks impassable at certain times of the year. Check with your travel agent or the individual tourist boards for information on the best times to visit the countries and areas you are interested in. Remember, too, that elephants are wild animals, however familiar they may seem from zoos, circuses, and wildlife films. Their size makes them dangerous to humans, and female elephants are fiercely protective of their young. Follow the instructions of your guide or tour operator regarding behavior around wild animals.

Some preparatory reading will enhance your experience of elephants in the wild. A few recommended books are Iain and Oria Douglas-Hamilton's *Among the Elephants,* Cynthia Moss's *Elephant Memories: Thirteen Years in the Life of an Elephant Family,* and Heathcote Williams's *Sacred Elephant.*

WAYS YOU CAN HELP

The World Wildlife Fund suggests the following six ways individuals can contribute to the conservation of elephants:

1. Help reduce the demand for ivory by not buying it.

2. Support the zoo in your community and find out what it is doing to help conserve elephants. Many zoos sponsor "Elephant Days" to help raise money and public awareness about elephants. Volunteer to help these efforts.

3. Write letters to your members of Congress and urge them to support appropriations for the African Elephant Conservation Act and international agreements such as the Convention on International Trade in Endangered Species (CITES). Let your representatives know that you are concerned about the future of the African and Asian elephants!

4. Send letters to the editor of your local paper that describe the plight of the elephant and the role we can play to help protect them.

5. Check the merchandise in the department store in your area. If ivory is for sale, contact the store management and let them know that you oppose the sale of elephant ivory!

6. Learn all you can about the elephant and tell others what you have learned. Encourage people not to buy ivory.

Citizens of countries other than the United States can accomplish the same goals by contacting the appropriate authorities in their own countries.

Now that an international ban on the ivory trade is in force, three additional actions may also be of help:

1. If you already own ivory, don't glamorize it by wearing it. As the poaching of walruses in the Bering Strait proves, an appetite for ivory still lingers in the public taste. It's all too easy to forget that a beautiful piece of ivory jewelry almost always means that an elephant has been butchered by poachers.

2. Visit countries that have elephant populations and want to protect them. Tourism is an important economic sector in many developing nations, and part of the hard currency you bring into the nations of Africa and Asia will be channeled into local conservation programs.

3. Contribute to organizations that sponsor elephant conservation programs. For many developing nations, the time when their conservation programs will be self-supporting is still many years away. Here are some organizations that make grants in support of elephant conservation:

World Wildlife Fund
1250 Twenty-fourth Street, NW
Washington, DC 20037

African Wildlife Foundation
1717 Massachusetts Avenue, NW
Washington, DC 20036

International Union for the Conservation of Nature
Regional Office/Eastern Africa
P.O. Box 68200
Nairobi, Kenya

David Sheldrick Wildlife Trust
P.O. Box 15555
Nairobi, Kenya

Make checks payable to the organization of your choice and specify that the money is to go toward helping elephants. Each organization can provide you with information on the tax status of your gifts.

BIBLIOGRAPHY

Allens, Buff Mshamba. "Ivory Prices Low—Leakey." *The Standard* (March 30, 1990): 9.

Allman, William F. with Joannie M. Schrof. "Can They Be Saved?" *U.S. News & World Report,* 107 (October 2, 1989): 52-58.

————. "Not Just Blowing Their Horns." *U.S. News & World Report,* 104 (May 9, 1988): 68.

Beard, Peter. *The End of the Game,* revised edition. San Francisco: Chronicle Books, 1988.

Booth, William. "Africa Is Becoming an Elephant Graveyard." *Science,* 243 (February 10, 1989): 732.

Boynton, Graham. "Slaughter of the Herds." *Condé Nast Traveler* (September 1989): 140-151, 164-170.

Cameron, Kenneth M. *Into Africa: A Social History of the East African Safari.* Wellingborough, England: Equation Books, 1990.

Cherfas, Jeremy. "Decision Time on African Ivory Trade." *Science,* 246 (October 6, 1989): 26-27.

————. "Science Gives Ivory a Sense of Identity." *Science,* 246 (December 1, 1989): 1120-1121.

Dinerstein, Eric. "Nepal's 'Landrovers' Cover Themselves with Dust and Glory." *Smithsonian* 19 (September 1988): 70-80.

Douglas-Hamilton, Iain and Oria Douglas-Hamilton. *Among the Elephants.* New York: The Viking Press, 1975.

Eltringham, S.K. *Elephants.* Poole, England: Blandford Press, 1982.

Freeman, Dan. *Elephants: The Vanishing Giants.* New York: G. P. Putnam's Sons, 1981.

Gucwa, David and James Ehmann. *To Whom It May Concern: An Investigation of the Art of Elephants.* New York: W. W. Norton & Co., 1985.

Gup, Ted. "Trail of Shame." *Time,* 134 (October 16, 1989): 66-77.

Holman, Dennis. *The Elephant People.* London: John Murray, 1967.

Holman, Dennis with Eric Rundgren. *Inside Safari Hunting.* London: W. H. Allen, 1969.

Klingender, Winifred and Evelyn Antal. *Animals in Art and Thought to the End of the Middle Ages.* Cambridge, MA: MIT Press, 1971.

Lamb, David. *The Africans.* New York: Vintage Books, 1987.

Linden, Eugene. "Last Stand for Africa's Elephants." *Time,* 133 (February 20, 1989): 76-77.

Melland, Frank Hulme. *Elephants in Africa.* London: Country Life, 1938.

Moss, Cynthia. *Elephant Memories: Thirteen Years in the Life of an Elephant Family.* New York: Fawcett Columbine, 1988.

Nzuma, Victor. "Rogue Jumbos on the Rampage." *Daily Nation* (April 2, 1990): 12.

Opanga, Kwendo. "Wildlife Crusade Bears Fruit." *Daily Nation* (April 25, 1990): 4.

Owen-Smith, R. Norman. *Megaherbivores.* New York: Press Syndicate of the University of Cambridge, 1988.

Payne, Katharine. "Elephant Talk." *National Geographic,* 176 (August 1989): 264-277.

Perlez, Jane. "African Wildlife Parks: Is Less Wild the Way of the Future?" *New York Times* (January 23, 1990): C4.

————. "Can He Save the Elephants?" *New York Times Magazine* (January 7, 1990): V128-33.

————. "A Puzzle for Zimbabwe: Too Many Elephants." *New York Times,* (November 14, 1989): A7.

Poole, Joyce H. "Elephants in Musth, Lust." *Natural History,* 96 (November 1987): 46-53.

————. "Elephant Trunk Calls." *Swara,* 11 (November/December 1988): 28-33.

Ransdell, Eric. "Heavy Artillery for Horns of Plenty." *U.S. News & World Report,* 106 (February 20, 1989): 61-64.

_____. "The Leakey Offensive." *Outside,* XV (January 1990): 36-41, 80.

Redmon, Ian. "Islands of Elephants." *Swara,* 10 (March/April 1987): 14-19.

Scullard, H. H. *The Elephant in the Greek and Roman World.* Ithaca, NY: Cornell University Press, 1974.

Seligman, Daniel. "Pachyderm Policy." *Fortune,* 120 (November 20, 1989): 235, 238.

Seligmann, Jean with Lynda Wright. "How To Handle an Elephant." *Newsweek,* 112 (November 14, 1988): 71.

Sikes, Sylvia K. *The Natural History of the African Elephant.* London: Weidenfeld & Nicolson, 1971.

Simpson, George Gaylord. *Splendid Isolation: The Curious History of South American Mammals.* New Haven, CT: Yale University Press, 1980.

Stevens, William K. "Britain Exempts Hong Kong from Ivory Ban." *New York Times* (January 23, 1990): C5.

Tisdale, Sallie. "The Only Harmless Great Thing." *The New Yorker,* 64 (January 23, 1989): 38-48, 77-89.

Toynbee, J. M. C. *Animals in Roman Life and Art.* Ithaca, NY: Cornell University Press, 1973.

"Tusk, Tusk." *Time,* 133 (May 1989): 56.

"Why Zimbabwe Opposes Banning the Ivory Trade." *Swara,* 12 (September/October 1989): 8-9.

Williams, Heathcote. *Sacred Elephant.* New York: Harmony Books, 1989.

Western, David. "The Ecological Role of Elephants in Africa." *Pachyderm,* (No. 12, 1989): 42-45.

INDEX